perverts

Also from EATMS Productions

Books on power, survival, women's autonomy, and the systems shaping modern America.

Nonfiction

Billionaires, Capitalism, and Power

Evil and the Mountain Ungreed
Self Help for American Billionaires
Selfish Steve and the Ivory Tower
Tariffs, Taxes, & Face-Eating Leopards
Ban Billionaires: Fascism Fix

Fascism, Religion, and Cultural Control

Self Help for the Manosphere
Fascism 2025
Fascism & the Perverts & the Greed Virus
Christian Fascism Marriage Book
Tyranny, Table Manners, & Tiramisu

Guides for Women's Autonomy and Protection

How to Survive in Post-America as a Woman
Project 2025 American Drag
4B – Burn, Ban, Boycott, Build
4B OG – So No Go GYN
I'm Glad He's Dead

Analysis of Authoritarian Project 2025

Project 2025: The Blueprint
Project 2025: The List
Project 2025, Christian Dumb Dumbs, & The Republican Agenda
Fascism, Project 2025, & The Pinkprint

Modern Rewrites for Women

Stoic Principles Reimagined
Siddhartha Reimagined
The Prince Reimagined for Women
The Art of War Reimagined for Women
The Jungle Reimagined
The Constitution Reimagined for Women

Machine Learning Series

AI, Bitcoin, Nostr for Women
AI, Safety, & Security for Women
AI, Anxiety, & Health for Women
AI, Kids, & Family Safety for Women
AI, Creativity, & Personal Expression for Women
AI, Independent Work, & Parallel Power for Women

Social Systems Series

Emotional Labor for Women
Household Power for Women
Workplace Power for Women
Medical Bias for Women
Aging Systems for Women
Recovery Systems for Women

Fiction

Dystopian Stories of Resistance and Collapse

Propaganda Paige & the Missing Prosperity
Propaganda Paige & the TIDE Manifesto
Propaganda Paige & the Shadow Cartographers
Propaganda Paige & the Prosperity Alliance
Propaganda Paige & the Shattered Truth
Propaganda Paige & the Rising TIDE
Propaganda Paige & the Last Bastion
Propaganda Paige & the Dawn of Prosperity
Project 2025: Dorian — The Last Men
Project 2025: Boy — A Last Men Novel

Fascism
& the
perverts
& the
Greed Virus
Call Out Culture 2

by
Eve Macrae

EATMS
PRODUCTIONS

ISBN 978-1-966014-14-0

Cover, interior design, interior prints by: Esme Mees

eatms@pm.me
www.eatms.me

Check out EATMS Underground:
https://tinyurl.com/eatmsNOSTR

Printed in the United States of America.

Bunch together a group of people deliberately chosen for strong religious feelings, and you have a practical guarantee of dark morbidities expressed in crime, perversion, and insanity.

— H. P. Lovecraft

Table of Contents

Introduction
Welcome to the Croag (½ cockroach ½ frog) Carnival

Fascism in the 21st century isn't a stormtrooper marching down Main Street, it's a sleazy, bloated carnival rolling into town, selling snake oil and broken dreams while rigging every game on the midway. The strongmen and barkers of this grotesque sideshow aren't just the jackbooted thugs of yesteryear; they've traded in their uniforms for tailored suits, yachts, and private jets. These modern-day ringmasters, billionaires, fascist politicians, and self-righteous Christian nationalists, have turned society into their personal funhouse, twisting every value, law, and institution to reflect their own warped appetites. They sip overpriced whiskey on superyachts docked next to other yachts, their obscene wealth towering like gilded monuments to their unchecked greed, while the rest of the world drowns in rising seas and crushing poverty. It's not just about control anymore; it's about perverting the very notion of decency and freedom. They gorge themselves on public resources, strip away basic rights, and then laugh in our faces, calling it "freedom" as the fires of their greed consume everything.

These aren't just your run-of-the-mill bad guys. No, these are the ultimate perverts, twisting morality, democracy, and society itself into something grotesque. They scream about "family values" while defending laws that allow child marriage. They claim to protect children while turning a blind eye to sexual abuse in schools, churches, and sports teams. They elevate serial rapists, domestic abusers, and adulterers as paragons of leadership, rewarding them with more power for their crimes.

They call themselves defenders of freedom while dismantling every system that allows people to live with dignity. It's a sickening carnival where their hypocrisy isn't just tolerated, it's celebrated. They've taken the sacred and turned it into a freak show, where every banner of justice or equality is torn down and replaced with the lurid neon signs of their exploitation and lies.

What makes it all so unbearable is how normal they've made it feel. They've convinced us that this dystopian circus is just the way things are. The billionaire who builds a pipeline through sacred lands and destroys ecosystems is hailed as a "job creator." The politician who blocks legislation to protect women and children from violence is re-elected with applause. The theocrat who dismantles reproductive rights is called a "defender of life." They've mastered the art of gaslighting, of making the grotesque seem holy and the absurd seem logical. They manipulate the narrative so thoroughly that their perversions become invisible, woven into the fabric of everyday life. This is their greatest trick: they've built a carnival of horrors and sold it to us as the American Dream. And the worst part? We've all been forced to buy a ticket.

Don't be fooled, this carnival isn't some harmless distraction. It's a finely tuned machine of oppression and exploitation, designed to distract, divide, and drain us while they rake in the profits. Every tent is rigged: healthcare, housing, education, labor. They break these systems on purpose, then point to the wreckage and say, "See? Government doesn't work. Let's privatize it!" But privatization doesn't mean freedom, it means less choice, higher costs, and more control in their hands. They profit off the misery they engineer, trapping us in endless cycles of exploitation. It's like a grotesque amusement park where the only ride is a rollercoaster of despair, and they're the ones collecting the admission fees.

These perverts don't stop at exploiting the system, they rewrite the rules to ensure no one else can ever play. They hoard
10

wealth and flaunt it like trophies: yachts for their yachts, private jets for their pets, and tax breaks for themselves while the rest of us scrape by. They aren't just rich, they're obscenely, unapologetically, cartoonishly rich. And with that wealth comes power, which they use to bend society to their will. They demand to inspect girls' private parts in locker rooms under the guise of "fairness" while ignoring rampant abuse in their own circles. They protect laws that allow child marriage because it suits their sick patriarchal fantasies. They weaponize religion, twisting scripture to justify their sociopathic tendencies, declaring themselves "ordained by God" while dismantling freedoms America was literally founded to protect.

And the hypocrisy, it's endless. They claim to love freedom but scream for privatization, stripping away our choices and rights. They cry about "censorship" while silencing anyone who calls out their abuses. They claim to stand for "law and order" while turning the criminal justice system into a tool for exploiting people of color and protecting their cronies. They've turned hypocrisy into an art form, their lies so bold and brazen that they dare you to challenge them. And if you do? They double down, gaslighting you into questioning your own reality.

This isn't just greed, it's an insatiable hunger to dominate, control, and corrupt everything that doesn't serve them. They're not just perverts in the sense of personal depravity, they're perverts of society, morality, and democracy itself. They won't stop until the entire world is a reflection of their grotesque appetites, where freedom is just another word for exploitation, and justice is reserved for those who can afford it.

But here's the thing: they only win if we let them. They thrive on our exhaustion, our silence, and our belief that nothing can change. They've built this carnival of greed and lies, but it doesn't have to stay open forever. This book isn't just an exposé, it's a call to arms. It's a reminder that we outnumber them, that we have the power to fight back. They want us to feel powerless because that's how they keep their carnival running. But we're here to tell you: the show's over. It's time to shut it down. Let's tear down the tents, expose the rigged games, and burn the whole thing to the ground. They've had their time, we're taking it back.

Their perversions extend far beyond personal depravity and seep into every systemic crack they can find, transforming laws, institutions, and basic human decency into tools for their own grotesque agenda. They don't just protect rapists and abusers, they elevate them, turning predators into "pillars of society," granting them authority over the very people they harm. The powerful are shielded while survivors are silenced, their trauma dismissed as inconvenient noise in the machine of control. Domestic abuse protections? Too "woke" for their liking. Reproductive rights? Sacrificed on the altar of "family values," a term they've warped into a cruel joke. They dress up oppression as morality, stripping women and children of every safeguard while patting themselves on the back for their so-called virtue.

Meanwhile, their exploitation knows no bounds. They mock and degrade people of color, turning the criminal justice system into a conveyor belt for free labor. Under the guise of "law and order," they feed this machine with the lives and futures of the marginalized. It's modern-day slavery, wrapped in patriotic slogans and legal jargon, sold to the public as necessary for safety and security. And let's not forget how they champion "freedom" when it's their own, screaming for privatization while they destroy every public system that gives ordinary people a chance. Healthcare? Gutted and handed to corporate cronies. Education? Stripped bare and turned into a pay-to-play scheme where the rich thrive, and everyone else is left behind. They break these systems on purpose, then smugly point to the wreckage and say, "See? Government doesn't work!" Their endgame is always the same: less choice, less freedom, and more control concentrated in their greedy, perverse hands.

And then there's the truly twisted part, their religious perversions. These are the theocrats who preach about morality from gilded pulpits, all while building golden idols to greed, power, and exploitation. They twist scripture into a weapon, wielding it against anyone who dares to challenge their authority. They declare themselves "ordained by God," using religion as a shield to mask their sociopathic tendencies. They don't care about the teachings of Christ or any other semblance of faith, they care about control, about bending religion to justify their authoritarian ambitions. They want a theocratic state where their twisted desires are enshrined as law, where their sociopathy is canonized as divine truth. They scream about protecting "religious freedom," but what they really mean is their freedom to oppress, exploit, and destroy in the name of God.

Their hypocrisy is boundless, their gaslighting relentless. They break the government, then smugly point to the shattered pieces and say, "See? This is why we need private control." They cry about freedom while stripping it away from everyone else. They demand accountability for others while escaping justice themselves. They scream about censorship while silencing anyone who disagrees with them. Their entire existence is a mockery of morality, a grotesque parody of leadership, an insult to every value they claim to uphold. These perverts are not just corrupt, they are the architects of corruption, reveling in their ability to destroy everything good and decent while convincing the world they're doing us all a favor.

This isn't just about greed. This is something far darker, a deranged obsession with domination and control, a pathological drive to annihilate anything that challenges their twisted sense of entitlement. They don't just want to rule; they want to warp the world into their grotesque vision of what it means to lead. They are the perverts of morality, society, and democracy itself, and they won't stop until every corner of this planet reflects their diseased ambitions.

Let's not sugarcoat this. If you're reading this, you already know something is deeply, fundamentally wrong with the world we're living in. And you're right, it is. What you're about to dive into isn't just a book; it's a battle cry, a demand that we stop letting these socio-economic, religious predators have their way. These perverts, because that's what they are, have taken everything good and decent and twisted it into something grotesque for their own gain. They've perverted morality, democracy, freedom, and even religion to suit their endless hunger for power and profit. They don't want a better world, they want a world where they own everything, control everyone, and crush anyone who dares to get in their way.

And here's the truth: they thrive because we let them. They bet on your exhaustion, your silence, your apathy. They bet on you feeling powerless because that's how they win. But here's the thing, they only win if we let them. We outnumber them. We have the power to fight back. They want you to think it's hopeless, that they've already won. But they're wrong. This isn't their world to take, it's ours to defend.

This is your invitation, your rallying cry, your call to arms. It's time to fight back. Refuse to accept their carnival of control as the new normal. Expose their lies, dismantle their power, and tear down the grotesque systems they've built. The world doesn't have to be this way. But it starts with us, with all of us refusing to play by their rules. It starts here, with you. They've had their show, now it's time to shut it down. Let's get to work.

The Greed Virus Defined

For the purpose of this book, and, frankly, life moving forward, let's stop pretending this is anything other than what it is: a Greed Virus. That's right, folks, it's a full-blown pandemic of its own, and unlike other viruses, this one doesn't just hit individuals. No, this sickness infects systems, institutions, governments, and entire cultures. It's a voracious disease, eating through morality, decency, and justice with the singular, sociopathic goal of devouring everything it touches. If you've ever wondered why things feel so rigged, why the rich keep getting richer while the rest of us are left fighting for scraps, well, here's your answer. It's not a bug in the system; it's the system itself, infected by this all-consuming virus.

Let's be clear: the Greed Virus doesn't stop with personal greed. It's not just about the billionaire who buys yachts for his yachts or the politician stuffing their pockets behind closed doors. This is systemic greed, a coordinated effort to warp every institution, healthcare, education, labor, housing, into a cash cow for those who already have more than enough. This virus doesn't just harm; it mutates. It turns morality into profit margins, community into division, and democracy into a grotesque parody of itself, where the only real vote that matters comes from a fat check with a billionaire's name on it.

But here's the kicker: the Greed Virus thrives in moments of crisis. Look no further than the pandemic, a time when people were dying by the thousands, scared and desperate for stability. What did the infected do? Did they step up to help? Of course not. They smelled an opportunity. While essential workers risked their lives and families mourned loved ones, the hosts of the Greed Virus, corporations, billionaires, and, yes, our so-called leaders, were lining their pockets. Remember greedflation? Prices for basic goods like groceries and gas skyrocketed, and we were told it was just "market forces" or "supply chain issues." But let's not mince words here: it was profiteering, plain and simple. They jacked up prices because they could, knowing full well that people had no choice but to pay. While the world burned, they cashed in.

And where were our politicians during all this? Oh, they were busy stuffing their own pockets. Let's not kid ourselves, these aren't public servants. They're donors' servants, loyal only to the corporations and billionaires who bankroll their campaigns. Instead of regulating industries or demanding accountability, they were too busy protecting the profits of their puppet masters. And when they weren't outright complicit, they were busy distracting us with culture wars, hoping we wouldn't notice the handouts they were giving to the wealthiest among us. It's disgusting, but it's also exactly what we've come to expect in a system so thoroughly corrupted by the Greed Virus.

But let's get something straight: this isn't some natural disaster or an inevitable part of human nature. The Greed Virus is a choice. Every billionaire hoarding wealth, every CEO exploiting workers, every politician turning a blind eye, they're all making an active decision to perpetuate this sickness. It's not that they can't stop; it's that they don't want to. The suffering of others isn't a bug in their system; it's the point. They profit off pain, inequality, and exploitation, and they do it with a smug sense of entitlement that's as infuriating as it is grotesque. So, let's be crystal clear: they deserve no quarter, no pity, and no excuses. This isn't some tragic inevitability, it's a malicious, calculated act, and they should be treated accordingly.

Take healthcare, for example. While millions were losing their jobs and their access to basic medical care during the pandemic, what were health insurance companies doing? Raking in record profits, of course. They jacked up premiums, denied coverage, and cut corners, all while CEOs collected obscene bonuses. And what did our politicians do? Did they step in to rein in this exploitation? Nope. They let it happen because their campaigns were bankrolled by the very corporations profiting off people's desperation. The Greed Virus doesn't just infect corporations; it infects the governments meant to regulate them. It turns public institutions into tools of exploitation, where laws are written not to protect people but to shield profits.

And let's not forget education. Public schools are underfunded, teachers are overworked, and students are drowning in debt. Meanwhile, private institutions and for-profit colleges rake in billions, turning education into a commodity accessible only to those who can afford it. This isn't a coincidence; it's a deliberate choice made by the infected hosts of the Greed Virus. They see education not as a public good but as another opportunity to exploit and profit. And the politicians? They're more concerned with banning books and policing bathrooms than addressing the systemic inequality that keeps generations trapped in cycles of poverty.

So what's the antidote? First, recognition. We have to call this what it is: a manufactured sickness designed to enrich the few at the expense of the many. Second, resistance. We can't afford to accept this as normal anymore. And third, refusal. Refusal to let them gaslight us into thinking their greed is inevitable, that their exploitation is just "how the world works." It's not. It's a choice, and it's a choice we can fight.

The Greed Virus thrives in darkness, silence, and complacency. But like any virus, it can be stopped when enough people recognize the harm, break the cycle, and commit to building a world where justice and compassion, not greed, define what it means to thrive. This isn't just about surviving the system, it's about dismantling it, curing the sickness, and creating something better. Let's start here. Let's start now.

~1
Fascism Wears a Suit Now

The rise of Christian nationalism in the United States has become one of the most potent and dangerous drivers of modern fascism, entwined with GOP extremism to form a political and cultural force that has reshaped the nation's institutions and values. Christian nationalism is not merely an expression of religious identity or spirituality; it is a political ideology that seeks to merge Christianity, or at least a particular interpretation of it, with governance. It thrives on the idea that the United States was founded as a Christian nation and that its laws, culture, and leadership must reflect conservative Christian principles. This ideology has weaponized faith to impose a rigid, exclusionary vision of morality on the country, systematically eroding the rights and freedoms of those who do not conform.

Over the past two decades, the Republican Party has aligned itself almost entirely with this movement, adopting its rhetoric and legislative priorities. The GOP has become a willing vessel for Christian nationalism, using it to energize its base, consolidate power, and enforce its social agenda. This transformation has been accelerated by the party's shift toward extremism, rejecting traditional conservatism in favor of authoritarian tactics. What began as a calculated strategy to court evangelical voters has morphed into a full embrace of a far-right ideology that seeks to remake the United States into a theocratic state, where secularism, diversity, and dissent are cast as threats to national identity.

Central to the rise of Christian nationalism and GOP extremism is the systematic erosion of democratic norms and institutions. Republican politicians and their allies have embraced voter suppression as a primary tool to maintain power, targeting communities of color, young voters, and other groups less likely to support their agenda. Gerrymandering, voter ID laws, and purging voter rolls are just a few of the tactics employed to ensure that elections favor the GOP, regardless of the popular will. This deliberate manipulation of the democratic process reveals a fundamental truth about modern Republicanism: its survival depends not on winning the hearts and minds of the majority but on controlling the mechanisms of power.

This control has extended to the judiciary, with the Supreme Court emerging as a key driver of fascist policies in the United States. Over the past decade, the Court has been packed with conservative justices who align ideologically with Christian nationalism and the GOP's far-right agenda. These justices have delivered rulings that undermine civil liberties, dismantle protections for marginalized communities, and entrench corporate power at the expense of individual rights. The Court's decision to overturn *Roe v. Wade* in 2022 marked a pivotal moment in this trajectory, stripping away federal protections for abortion rights and opening the door for states to impose draconian restrictions. This ruling was not just about abortion; it signaled the Court's willingness to revisit and potentially dismantle other established rights, including access to contraception, same-sex marriage, and protections against discrimination.

The Supreme Court has also played a critical role in enabling voter suppression and cementing GOP control over the electoral process. In 2013, the Court's decision in *Shelby County v. Holder* gutted key provisions of the Voting Rights Act, effectively dismantling federal oversight of election laws in states with histories of racial discrimination. This decision emboldened Republican-led states to pass a wave of restrictive voting laws, disproportionately affecting Black and Brown communities. By weakening the legal framework that protects voting rights, the Court has not only undermined democracy but also reinforced the racial and economic hierarchies that Christian nationalism seeks to preserve.

One of the most troubling aspects of this judicial shift is the Supreme Court's increasing deference to corporate interests, which aligns seamlessly with the GOP's broader agenda. In cases like *Citizens United v. FEC*, the Court has expanded the influence of money in politics, allowing corporations and billionaires to wield disproportionate power in elections. This ruling, in particular, has paved the way for dark money to flood the political system, funding candidates, think tanks, and media campaigns that advance Christian nationalist and GOP objectives. The result is a political landscape where corporate interests and far-right ideologies converge, creating a feedback loop that prioritizes profit and power over people.

The intersection of Christian nationalism, GOP extremism, and Supreme Court rulings represents a coordinated assault on the foundational principles of American democracy. These forces work in tandem to strip away the separation of church and state, entrench minority rule, and legitimize authoritarianism under the guise of constitutionalism. This strategy is deeply insidious because it cloaks fascist policies in the language of democracy and freedom, making them harder to challenge. Christian nationalists frame their efforts as a defense of religious liberty, even as they seek to impose their beliefs on others. GOP extremists claim to be protecting the integrity of elections, even as they manipulate the process to their advantage. The Supreme Court presents its rulings as interpretations of the Constitution, even as they erode the very freedoms the document was designed to protect.

At the heart of this assault is a relentless drive to consolidate power by any means necessary. The cruelty and barbarism of these policies are not unintended consequences, they are the point. Banning abortion, stripping away voting rights, and privileging corporations over individuals serve to reinforce a hierarchy where power is concentrated in the hands of a wealthy, predominantly white, and predominantly male elite. This hierarchy is sustained by a narrative that demonizes the "other," whether that means immigrants, LGBTQ+ individuals, or anyone who challenges the status quo. The result is a society where fear and division are weaponized to maintain control, leaving little room for dissent or solidarity.

The rise of Christian nationalism and GOP extremism in the United States is not an isolated phenomenon; it is part of a global trend toward authoritarianism. However, the unique characteristics of the American context, its history of slavery and segregation, its deeply entrenched religious culture, and its outsized influence on the world stage, make this iteration particularly dangerous. The fusion of religious fundamentalism with political extremism creates a volatile cocktail that threatens not only the United States but also the global fight for democracy and human rights.

The Supreme Court's role in this dynamic cannot be overstated. By positioning itself as an arbiter of constitutional law while consistently advancing a far-right agenda, the Court has become a tool of authoritarianism rather than a check on it. Its decisions are shaping a nation where rights are conditional, democracy is hollow, and power is increasingly concentrated in the hands of a few. This is not an abstract threat; it is a lived reality for millions of Americans who find themselves increasingly marginalized, disenfranchised, and dehumanized.

And yet, understanding this reality is the first step toward dismantling it. The rise of Christian nationalism, GOP extremism, and a far-right Supreme Court is not inevitable, it is the result of deliberate choices made by those in power. Recognizing these patterns, calling out their impact, and mobilizing against them are essential to reclaiming the democratic ideals that are under siege. Fascism may thrive on cruelty and division, but it is not invincible. Its strength lies in its ability to overwhelm, but its weakness lies in its reliance on a system that can be exposed, disrupted, and ultimately replaced.

The fusion of Christian nationalism, GOP extremism, and an activist Supreme Court has created a self-reinforcing cycle of oppression, one that continues to consolidate power in fewer hands while dismantling the mechanisms of accountability. This system isn't just attacking the present; it is actively rewriting the past and future of the United States. From erasing the gains of the civil rights movement to nullifying decades of progress on reproductive rights, the alliance between these forces is dragging the nation into a regressive, authoritarian state. Yet, what makes this even more insidious is their ability to operate under the veneer of legitimacy, wielding the Constitution and the democratic process as shields for their anti-democratic agenda.

Christian nationalism in particular provides the moral and cultural framework for these policies. Its proponents have skillfully co-opted religious language to frame their authoritarian vision as a divine mandate. By positioning themselves as warriors in a culture war against secularism, diversity, and progressivism, they justify policies that strip rights from marginalized groups while privileging their own narrow interpretation of morality. This isn't about faith, it's about power. Faith is merely the tool used to silence opposition, to claim moral superiority, and to mask the violence of their agenda. It's a strategy as old as history itself, and in the hands of modern Christian nationalists, it has become a weapon of mass control.

This weapon is wielded by the GOP with alarming precision. Republican politicians at every level, from state legislatures to Congress, have become the enforcers of this agenda. They have embraced a politics of cruelty, reveling in policies that harm immigrants, LGBTQ+ communities, women, and people of color. Whether it's passing draconian anti-abortion laws, enacting "Don't Say Gay" bills, or criminalizing gender-affirming healthcare, the GOP's legislative priorities are driven by a clear goal: to erase the existence of anyone who challenges their vision of a white, Christian, patriarchal America.

At the same time, the GOP has weaponized grievance and fear to maintain its base, creating a perpetual state of cultural hysteria. Every election is framed as an existential battle for the "soul of the nation," every policy disagreement as a fight between good and evil. This constant escalation ensures that their supporters remain loyal, even as the policies enacted in their name serve only to enrich the powerful and entrench inequality. The irony is painful: the very people harmed most by GOP policies are often the ones most fervently defending them, convinced by decades of propaganda that their suffering is noble or necessary for the greater good.

The Supreme Court has proven to be the perfect partner in this effort. While Congress remains gridlocked and the executive branch subject to frequent changes in leadership, the Court operates as a steady hand advancing far-right priorities. Its conservative majority, cemented by lifetime appointments, ensures that even as public opinion shifts toward progressive ideals, the laws of the land move in the opposite direction. This is the essence of minority rule: using unelected bodies to impose policies that would never survive in a truly democratic process. And because the Court cloaks its rulings in the language of constitutional interpretation, it grants a veneer of legitimacy to decisions that are fundamentally undemocratic.

Consider the Court's recent decisions, which have systematically dismantled safeguards designed to protect the most vulnerable. In addition to overturning *Roe v. Wade*, the Court has eroded environmental protections, upheld discriminatory immigration policies, and restricted the federal government's ability to regulate industries that endanger public health and safety. These decisions reveal a pattern: the Court consistently sides with corporations, religious institutions, and conservative political interests at the expense of individuals and communities. Each ruling chips away at the public's ability to challenge power, creating a landscape where the wealthy and well-connected are untouchable while the rest of society is left to fend for itself.

This dynamic is not an accident; it is by design. The GOP's decades-long project to reshape the judiciary, led by organizations like the Federalist Society, has paid off in spades. By flooding the courts with conservative judges, the GOP has created a legal system that prioritizes ideology over justice, ensuring that even if Republicans lose elections, their policies will endure. This is the long game of authoritarianism: control the courts, and you control the future.

The impact of this strategy is devastating. It's not just that people are losing rights; it's that they are losing hope. When the highest court in the land repeatedly upholds policies that harm the majority while privileging the elite, it sends a clear message: the system is rigged. This demoralization is a key feature of the current fascist project. By making people feel powerless, they hope to stifle resistance, ensuring that the machinery of oppression continues unchallenged.

Yet, if there is one thing history has shown us, it is that fascists overreach. Their cruelty, their barbarism, their unrelenting drive to dominate, it always becomes their weakness. They believe that by controlling the courts, the media, and the government, they can control the people. But they underestimate the power of the many. They underestimate the righteous anger of those who refuse to be silenced. They underestimate the inevitability of opposition. Because while they may seem insurmountable, their power is fragile. It depends on obedience, on silence, on people accepting the lie that nothing can change.

But something *can* change. We are not bound by their rules. We are not playing their game. The rise of Christian nationalism and GOP extremism, bolstered by an activist Supreme Court, is a wake-up call, not just to resist but to replace. The power they wield is real, but it is not absolute. It is built on a system that can be dismantled, disrupted, and reimagined. We are not powerless, and we are not alone. We are the many. We are the danger. We are the future. And we are ready.

It will take all of us. Each of us, in our own ways, fighting back every day, in every way, to reclaim what they have taken and to build what they've destroyed. For fifty years, they worked methodically to dismantle this country, rolling back rights for anyone who isn't rich, white, and male, dragging us backwards into an era of inequality and exploitation. They've chipped away at our democracy, turned us into a laughingstock of the free world, and rendered this so-called "land of the free" into something closer to a failed state. A shithole nation. But we don't have fifty years to reverse their damage, and we can't afford to waste another five minutes waiting for someone else to save us.

No cavalry is coming. No deus ex machina will swoop in to rescue us. The truth is harsh but liberating: *we are the change we've been waiting for.* This is on us. We are the ones who will shape the future, not politicians, not billionaires, not saviors, but us. It will be hard. It will take time. But gradually, and then suddenly, we will turn the tide. Just as they took decades to erode our rights and rig the system in their favor, we will work every day to undo their damage and build something better. We will use the tools of today to shape the tomorrow we want and deserve, because without us, there may not even *be* a tomorrow.

They don't believe in tomorrow. They don't believe in science. They've built a worldview so infected by greed that they've stopped caring about the future entirely. These parasitic frauds,

26

posing as Christians, patriots, and leaders, are nothing more than the festering symptoms of a greater sickness: greed. It's a disease that prioritizes profit over people, destruction over creation, and domination over humanity. It's a sickness that has metastasized into our courts, our government, and our culture.

But we are the cure. We who believe in science, in humanity, in the power of community and creativity, we are here to cauterize this wound. We will cordon off the infection and begin the slow, necessary work of healing the patient: Earth, humanity, and the American Dream itself. Because that dream, of equality, freedom, and opportunity, has been hijacked by the greedy few who have turned it into a nightmare for the rest of us. Healing America means reclaiming that dream, not just for ourselves but for everyone. It won't be easy. Healing never is. But it's possible. And thanks to us, it's inevitable. Fair is fair.

~2
Perverts in High Places

Let's not mince words: billionaires, fascists, and political elites
are masters of perversion, not just in the personal, scandalous
sense, but in a systemic, calculated way that undermines the
very foundations of decency and justice. They are not content
with simple greed or the hoarding of obscene wealth; no, they
need to warp the rules of society itself to reflect their twisted
values. They reward rapists, elevate serial abusers, and
normalize adultery and betrayal, not because these are
accidents of the system, but because this behavior mirrors their
own grotesque worldview. The pattern is clear: power protects
its own, and the most corrupt rise to the top because the system
is rigged to reward the predators, the exploiters, and the
destroyers.

Start with their ongoing defense of rapists and serial abusers.
How many times have we seen powerful men accused of
heinous acts against women and children, only to emerge
unscathed or, worse, rewarded? From the boardrooms of
Fortune 500 companies to the halls of Congress, these men are
given golden parachutes, cushy promotions, or platforms to
further their influence. A corporate executive is accused of
harassing employees? He resigns with a multi-million-dollar
severance package and ends up on the board of another
company within the year. A politician is exposed for a pattern
of sexual assault? He deflects, denies, and eventually shifts the
blame onto "cancel culture," returning to office as if nothing
happened. These individuals don't just avoid consequences,
they're emboldened. Their power not only shields them from

accountability but sends a clear message: this is the cost of doing business in a world infected by the Greed Virus.

This systemic indulgence of predators extends beyond the corporate and political arenas. Let's talk about child marriage. In 2025 America, there are still states that allow children as young as 10 to marry with parental consent. Who benefits from these archaic and morally bankrupt laws? The same elites who champion "family values" while quietly pushing back against reforms to outlaw this grotesque practice. Child marriage is not just a relic of the past; it's a tool of patriarchal control, a mechanism to exploit vulnerable young girls under the guise of tradition. Politicians who claim to stand for morality and decency routinely block attempts to raise the legal age for marriage. They argue, laughably, that it's about "freedom" and "parental rights," but let's be real: it's about preserving a system where the powerful can prey on the powerless without consequence.

And it doesn't stop there. These same politicians and elites actively work to repeal protections for women and girls, whether it's gutting laws against domestic abuse or dismantling reproductive rights. Domestic abuse protections are dismissed as "woke" policies, as if protecting women from violence is somehow an affront to traditional values. And let's not forget the assault on reproductive rights, where theocrats in suits hide behind the banner of "pro-life" while stripping away the autonomy of women and girls. They push draconian laws designed to control bodies and futures, framing their oppression as moral righteousness. The reality is far simpler: their goal is control, and they will exploit religion, tradition, and every other rhetorical tool to achieve it.

This isn't just a failure of morality, it's a deliberate choice to empower predators. The system doesn't just tolerate these behaviors; it rewards them. In a society where billionaires and political elites set the rules, their perversions become the norm. Adultery, for example, isn't just a personal failing for these men, it's practically a badge of honor. The more public their betrayals, the more they're seen as "alpha males" in certain circles. Serial adulterers are celebrated in the media, their infidelities framed as part of their charm or charisma. Never mind the destruction they leave in their wake, the broken families, the shattered trust, the public humiliation of their spouses and children. In their world, cheating is a symbol of dominance, another way to flaunt their power and disregard for societal norms.

Of course, the normalization of adultery and abuse is just the tip of the iceberg. These elites don't just break the rules, they rewrite them. They create systems that protect their actions and punish those who dare to speak out. Take non-disclosure agreements (NDAs), for instance. These legal tools are routinely weaponized to silence victims of harassment, assault, and abuse. NDAs ensure that predators can continue their behavior without fear of exposure, effectively turning the legal system into an accomplice to their crimes. And who writes these contracts? High-powered lawyers, corporate boards, and political operatives, all part of the same corrupt network that enables and rewards predatory behavior.

This brings us to the media, another cog in the machine that props up the grotesque behaviors of the powerful. Media outlets, often owned by billionaires or funded by corporate advertisers, rarely hold these elites accountable. Instead, they sanitize their stories, framing allegations of abuse or misconduct as mere "controversies" or "disputes." When a CEO is accused of harassment, the headline isn't "Executive Abuses Power"; it's "Company Faces PR Crisis." When a politician is exposed as a predator, the coverage focuses on the "political fallout" rather than the lives ruined by his actions. The media, whether through complicity or cowardice, becomes another shield for the predators, ensuring that the public never sees the full extent of their crimes.

But perhaps the most insidious aspect of this system is how it gaslights the public into accepting it. The language of "freedom" and "morality" is weaponized to justify the most grotesque behaviors. When a politician defends child marriage, he frames it as a matter of parental rights. When a CEO refuses to implement harassment training, she claims it's about protecting the company's "culture." These excuses are as hollow as they are infuriating, but they're effective because they tap into deeply ingrained societal myths about individualism, tradition, and authority. The elites know this, and they exploit it relentlessly.

And where does this leave us? In a society where the rules are written by predators for predators, where the most vulnerable are left to fend for themselves while the powerful feast on their labor, their bodies, and their futures. It's a grotesque carnival, a dystopian sideshow where the freaks aren't in the cages, they're running the whole damn thing. They've turned justice into a joke, morality into a marketing slogan, and freedom into a weapon to bludgeon the weak.

But let's not forget: this isn't just an accident of history or some natural state of affairs. This system was built, piece by piece, by the very people who benefit from it. They have chosen this path, knowing full well the harm it causes, because the suffering of others is the foundation of their power. They are not misguided; they are malicious. Their perversions aren't just personal failings, they're the building blocks of a society designed to protect the predators and punish the prey.

The first step in dismantling this grotesque system is to see it clearly, to name it for what it is, and to refuse to accept its lies any longer. These billionaires, fascists, and elites want us to believe their power is inevitable, their behavior excusable, their systems unchangeable. But none of that is true. The world they've built is a house of cards, propped up by our silence and complicity. It's time to knock it down.

If there's one thing billionaires, fascists, and political elites excel at, it's turning exploitation into an art form. Their systemic perversions aren't limited to abusing women and girls, they've perfected the grotesque science of exploiting people of color in labor markets and the criminal justice system while manipulating the public with cries of "freedom" and "morality." This is where their perversion moves beyond individuals and burrows into the very foundation of society, creating systems of control that are as insidious as they are effective. Their tools? Racism, fear-mongering, and the outright rewriting of history, all designed to gaslight the public into thinking this system is not only normal but somehow noble.

Let's start with labor markets. For generations, billionaires and their political cronies have used people of color as a disposable workforce, extracting as much labor as possible for as little compensation as they can get away with. They dress it up in the language of "opportunity" and "job creation," but the reality is far uglier. From agriculture to manufacturing to service industries, people of color have been forced into exploitative jobs with low wages, unsafe working conditions, and zero protections. Billionaire corporations like Amazon, for example, thrive on this model, building fortunes on the backs of workers, many of them immigrants or people of color, who are denied basic dignity. They're paid starvation wages while working brutal shifts in warehouses so meticulously engineered to maximize profit that bathroom breaks are considered a luxury. If they get injured or collapse from exhaustion, they're replaced without a second thought.

And the politicians? They're complicit. They pass laws to weaken unions, block minimum wage increases, and gut workplace safety regulations, all while raking in campaign donations from the very corporations they refuse to regulate. They gaslight the public by calling it "free-market economics" or "business-friendly policy," but let's call it what it is: exploitation. These policies aren't about creating opportunities;

they're about maintaining a labor force that's too desperate to demand fair treatment.

Of course, the exploitation doesn't stop with wages. The criminal justice system serves as another tool in their arsenal, turning people of color into commodities through mass incarceration. Private prisons, another brainchild of the Greed Virus, make billions by incarcerating Black and Brown bodies. These prisons don't just profit from filling cells; they've created a perverse economy where inmates are exploited for cheap labor, working for pennies an hour to manufacture goods or provide services for massive corporations. This isn't justice, it's modern-day slavery, wrapped in the flag of "law and order" and sold to the public as necessary for safety.

The pipeline to prison starts early. Communities of color are over-policed and under-resourced, with children funneled into the criminal justice system through discriminatory practices like school-to-prison pipelines. A minor infraction at school, a fight, a tardy, a harmless act of rebellion, is treated as a criminal offense when it happens in a predominantly Black or Brown neighborhood. The result? Entire generations of people of color are criminalized before they even reach adulthood, ensuring a steady supply of cheap labor for prisons and private industries alike.

Meanwhile, the politicians who oversee these systems have the audacity to claim they're protecting the public. They pander to fears of crime, often stoking racialized panic in suburban and rural areas, while ensuring the very policies they promote create the conditions for poverty and desperation. They gaslight the public with tough-on-crime rhetoric, painting themselves as saviors while perpetuating the same systemic injustices that make crime inevitable. And when people protest, when they rise up against police brutality and mass incarceration, what do these elites do? They double down. They demonize the protesters, call them radicals or anarchists, and unleash militarized police forces to suppress dissent. All the

34

while, the public is told it's about maintaining "order" and "security." The only thing being secured is the elite's stranglehold on power.

But their perversion doesn't stop at exploitation, it extends to how they rewrite history and manipulate narratives to justify their actions. They've turned gaslighting into a national sport, using it to erase the past and distort the present. When they exploit immigrant labor, they frame it as a win-win situation: the immigrants get "opportunity," and the corporations get a workforce willing to do jobs "Americans won't do." What they don't mention is how these same elites create the conditions that force people to immigrate in the first place, destabilizing economies and governments abroad through exploitation, trade agreements, and resource extraction. Then, once immigrants arrive, they are demonized as criminals or freeloaders while being worked to the bone in jobs that offer no path to stability or citizenship.

And the criminal justice system? They've rewritten that narrative, too. Mass incarceration isn't about racism or profit, they insist, it's about "safety" and "justice." They conveniently ignore the decades of data showing how systemic racism infects every level of policing and sentencing, leading to disproportionately harsh outcomes for people of color. They tell us the system isn't broken, it's just misunderstood. But that's the gaslighting at work: the system isn't broken at all. It's working exactly as intended, for them.

Their weaponization of "freedom" is perhaps their most grotesque perversion. These elites love to scream about liberty while simultaneously creating policies that strip it away from everyone else. They claim to champion "individual rights" while making it nearly impossible for people of color to live free from fear, poverty, or violence. They label attempts to address systemic racism ,whether through affirmative action, reparations, or criminal justice reform, as "attacks on freedom." The freedom they're so desperate to protect, it turns out, is their own freedom to exploit, oppress, and dominate.

Even their supposed "morality" is a farce. They wrap themselves in religious rhetoric, invoking God and family values to justify their actions. But let's look at their track record. Where are these "values" when corporations pay immigrant workers below minimum wage or fire them for taking a sick day? Where is this supposed morality when private prisons profit off incarcerating Black and Brown people for non-violent offenses? Their moral outrage is reserved for things like drag shows and gender-neutral bathrooms, while their own policies perpetuate cycles of poverty and violence. They cry about protecting the sanctity of life but gut funding for schools, healthcare, and housing in the same breath. It's hypocrisy so glaring it would be laughable if it weren't so devastating.

But perhaps the most insidious aspect of their gaslighting is how they convince the public that these systems are inevitable, even natural. They tell us that capitalism, with all its inequalities, is the only way forward. That policing, with all its brutality, is the only way to ensure safety. That incarceration, with all its racial bias, is the only way to maintain order. They frame any attempt to challenge these systems as radical, dangerous, or un-American. And too often, the public believes them, not because the lies are convincing, but because they're repeated so often and so loudly that they drown out dissent.

This is the true perversion: the ability to exploit, oppress, and gaslight with such precision that it becomes invisible to the very people it harms. These billionaires, fascists, and elites don't just control the system, they control the narrative, ensuring that their grotesque behavior is seen as necessary, even virtuous. They've built a society where their exploitation is normalized, their racism is justified, and their greed is celebrated.
But here's the truth: their power is an illusion. It relies on silence, complacency, and complicity. The moment we see through their lies, the moment we call out their perversions for

what they are, the foundation begins to crack. The machinery of exploitation can be dismantled, but it starts with recognizing the truth: this system was built by predators for predators, and it doesn't have to stay this way. The real freedom they fear isn't the freedom they claim to protect, it's ours, and it's time to take it back.

~3
The Greed Virus: Infection and Spread

The Greed Virus doesn't just live in boardrooms or behind closed political doors; it's out in the open, infecting the most basic aspects of life. It has transformed housing into a luxury item, work into exploitation, and the global economy into a playground for billionaires and corporations to exploit entire nations. This chapter explores how the virus targets systems and individuals alike, with devastating consequences for everyone but the wealthy elite.

The Housing Crisis as a Greed Playground

The Greed Virus has taken something as fundamental as housing, a basic human need, and turned it into one of its most profitable playgrounds. Shelter, which should be a universal right, has become a tool for billionaires and corporations to extract obscene amounts of wealth, often at the expense of the most vulnerable. The housing market has been commodified to the point where it no longer serves its original purpose of providing homes, it now serves as an investment vehicle for the wealthy, with devastating consequences for communities.

Take private equity firms, for example. These corporate giants aren't in the business of providing homes; they're in the business of squeezing as much profit as possible from housing. They buy up properties in bulk, often at bargain prices during economic downturns, and then jack up rents or sit on the properties until market prices skyrocket. Entire neighborhoods are gutted as families are priced out of their homes, replaced by high-income tenants or, worse, luxury developments that sit empty because they're marketed as speculative investments for other wealthy buyers.

Consider Blackstone, one of the world's largest private equity firms. During the aftermath of the 2008 financial crisis, a crisis caused, let's not forget, by Wall Street greed, Blackstone went on a buying spree, snapping up tens of thousands of foreclosed homes. Instead of helping rebuild communities, they turned those homes into rental properties, hiking rents to predatory levels. Families who had just lost their homes to foreclosure found themselves renting those very same houses from Blackstone at exorbitant rates. This wasn't just capitalism at work, it was a grotesque display of how the Greed Virus thrives on human suffering.

And it's not just private equity. Billionaires like Jeff Bezos and Elon Musk have their fingerprints all over this crisis, too. Companies like Amazon have driven up housing costs in cities like Seattle, where their corporate headquarters have turned once-affordable neighborhoods into overpriced enclaves for tech workers. Local families, unable to compete with the inflated demand, are pushed out, often with nowhere to go. Meanwhile, the billionaires at the helm of these corporations collect accolades for their "economic contributions" while the communities they've uprooted are left to pick up the pieces.

This commodification of housing has created a world where owning property is no longer about having a place to live, it's about wealth accumulation. Real estate is now a game for the rich, with homes treated as investment portfolios rather than places to raise families. Entire cities have become unaffordable, forcing people into overcrowded apartments, endless rent cycles, or, in the worst cases, homelessness. And the system is designed to ensure this dynamic doesn't change. Housing developers focus on luxury units, even in cities with housing shortages, because high-end developments yield the greatest returns. Affordable housing projects? They're an afterthought, if they're considered at all.

The result is a society where shelter, a basic human right, is denied to millions while the wealthy watch their property portfolios grow. It's not just unethical, it's systemic exploitation, fueled by the Greed Virus infecting every level of the housing market.

Labor Exploitation and the Greed Economy

If housing is the Greed Virus' playground, the labor market is its breeding ground. The virus has turned the global economy into a machine designed to extract as much value as possible from workers while giving them as little in return. From gig workers with no benefits to sweatshop laborers in developing countries, the Greed Virus thrives on exploitation.

Take the gig economy, for example. Companies like Uber and DoorDash market themselves as providing "flexible opportunities" for workers, but the reality is far more sinister. These companies classify their workers as independent contractors rather than employees, allowing them to skirt labor laws and avoid providing benefits like healthcare, sick leave, or a minimum wage. Drivers are forced to work long hours just to make ends meet, all while bearing the costs of fuel, vehicle maintenance, and insurance. And who profits? The executives and shareholders, who collect billions while their workers live paycheck to paycheck.

And then there's Amazon, the crown jewel of labor exploitation in the modern age. Jeff Bezos became the world's richest man during the pandemic, a time when Amazon's warehouse workers were risking their lives to meet skyrocketing demand. Stories of these workers urinating in bottles to avoid missing quotas or collapsing from exhaustion are not isolated incidents, they're features of a system designed to squeeze every ounce of productivity out of its workforce. Bezos added $70 billion to his net worth in 2020 alone, while many of his employees were forced to rely on food stamps to survive. This isn't innovation, it's exploitation, plain and simple.

But the Greed Virus doesn't stop at gig workers and warehouse employees. It spreads globally, targeting the most vulnerable populations in developing nations. Sweatshops in Bangladesh, for instance, churn out cheap clothing for Western consumers, with workers, mostly women, earning pennies an hour in unsafe conditions. The 2013 Rana Plaza disaster, where a garment factory collapsed and killed over 1,100 workers, was a direct result of this greed-driven system. The building was structurally unsound, but factory owners ignored safety warnings to keep production running. Why? Because profit margins mattered more than human lives.

And let's not forget how corporations exploit migrant workers. In agriculture, for example, undocumented immigrants are often forced to work under brutal conditions for meager pay, all while living in constant fear of deportation. These workers are essential to the food supply chain, yet they're treated as disposable. Meanwhile, the CEOs of the corporations profiting off their labor collect multi-million-dollar bonuses.

This isn't just a problem of individual greed, it's a systemic issue. Labor laws are deliberately weakened, unions are demonized, and workers are kept too overworked and underpaid to fight back. The Greed Virus has turned labor into a modern form of servitude, ensuring that the wealth flows upward while the people generating that wealth are left with crumbs.

The Greed Virus knows no borders. Its hosts, billionaires, corporations, and complicit governments, use globalization as a tool to extract wealth from developing nations, leaving destruction in their wake. This isn't globalization in the sense of cultural exchange or international cooperation, it's exploitation on a massive scale.

Consider how multinational corporations set up factories in countries with weak labor protections and low wages. They claim to be creating jobs and bringing "opportunity" to these regions, but the reality is far more exploitative. Workers in these factories are often paid below subsistence levels, forced to work grueling hours in unsafe conditions. And when the workers try to organize or demand better treatment? The corporations shut down the factories and move operations to another country, leaving entire communities in economic ruin.

Resource extraction is another glaring example. In resource-rich nations like the Democratic Republic of Congo, foreign corporations mine valuable materials like cobalt and coltan, essential for electronics, while leaving the local population in poverty. The environmental destruction caused by these operations is catastrophic, with rivers poisoned and ecosystems destroyed. And the profits? They flow to corporate executives and shareholders thousands of miles away, while the communities bearing the brunt of the destruction see none of the benefits.

Then there's the issue of debt. The International Monetary Fund (IMF) and World Bank, institutions ostensibly designed to help developing nations, often impose crippling debt conditions that force these countries to privatize public resources and cut social services. These austerity measures disproportionately harm the poor, while the wealthy, both locally and internationally, reap the rewards. It's a global system of exploitation, driven by the Greed Virus, that keeps wealth concentrated in the hands of the few while billions struggle to survive.

The global spread of the Greed Virus isn't just an economic issue, it's a moral one. It perpetuates inequality on a massive scale, ensuring that the people and nations with the least power are exploited the most. And as long as this system remains unchecked, the Greed Virus will continue to spread, consuming everything in its path.

The Greed Virus targets every aspect of life, from housing to labor to the global economy, turning systems designed to serve people into tools of exploitation. Its hosts, billionaires, corporations, and complicit governments, profit while millions suffer. But this isn't inevitable. It's a choice, and recognizing it as such is the first step toward fighting back. In the next part, we'll explore how this virus spreads even further, infecting culture, morality, and the planet itself.

The Greed Virus is relentless. It doesn't stop at housing, labor, or even the global economy. It reaches into the very fabric of culture, twisting societal values and reshaping morality into a grotesque justification for exploitation. It turns the environment, the planet we all depend on, into collateral damage in its endless pursuit of profit. The virus infects not just systems but hearts and minds, making greed appear normal, even aspirational. This is how it spreads further, corrupting everything it touches.

The Cultural Decay: Glorifying Greed and Dehumanizing Empathy

One of the most insidious effects of the Greed Virus is its ability to infect culture, reshaping societal values to align with its own twisted priorities. It glorifies wealth and materialism, erases empathy, and conditions people to see exploitation as just another part of life. This cultural shift doesn't happen overnight, it's the result of decades of propaganda from the

44

virus's most powerful hosts: corporations, billionaires, and the media they control.

Consider the way billionaires are portrayed in mainstream culture. They're not seen as hoarders of wealth or exploiters of systems; they're painted as geniuses, visionaries, and saviors. Look at how Elon Musk, Jeff Bezos, and Richard Branson are idolized for their space ventures. They're framed as pioneers, exploring the "final frontier," while conveniently ignoring that their wealth comes from squeezing workers, dodging taxes, and gutting the very Earth they're supposedly trying to escape. The Greed Virus rebrands them as heroes, distracting from the damage they cause.

At the same time, the virus dehumanizes those who suffer under its weight. Poverty is framed as a personal failing rather than a systemic issue. The poor are labeled lazy, unmotivated, or undeserving, while the rich are celebrated for their supposed hard work and ingenuity. This narrative erases the structural factors, like exploitative labor practices and skyrocketing housing costs, that keep people trapped in cycles of poverty. It's a deliberate effort to justify inequality and ensure that those at the bottom blame themselves, not the system.

The media plays a central role in spreading this cultural infection. Reality shows like *Shark Tank* glorify ruthless business practices, teaching audiences that the end justifies the means as long as there's profit. Social media platforms amplify influencers who flaunt their wealth, turning conspicuous consumption into a cultural ideal. Meanwhile, stories about workers striking for fair wages or tenants protesting against evictions are buried or dismissed as fringe issues. The Greed Virus dominates the narrative, ensuring that the values of exploitation and materialism are seen as the norm.

The Greed Virus doesn't just manipulate culture, it twists morality itself. It weaponizes religion, ethics, and social norms to frame greed as a virtue and systemic abuse as an unfortunate necessity. Nowhere is this more apparent than in the rise of Christian nationalism and its role in justifying policies that harm the vulnerable.

Christian nationalism, infected by the Greed Virus, has turned faith into a tool for legitimizing exploitation. It preaches a prosperity gospel that equates wealth with divine favor, teaching followers that the rich are chosen by God while the poor are simply suffering the consequences of their own failures. This theology isn't just harmful, it's heretical. It ignores the teachings of Christ, who spoke of compassion for the poor, the dangers of wealth, and the moral imperative to care for the least among us. Yet it's pushed by megachurch pastors and televangelists who live in mansions funded by donations from their congregants, many of whom are struggling to make ends meet.

The Greed Virus also uses morality to attack those who challenge it. Striking workers are painted as greedy; activists demanding environmental protections are labeled extremists. This inversion of morality allows the powerful to frame themselves as the victims, even as they exploit others. Billionaires, for example, claim they're being "punished" by taxes, despite benefiting from loopholes that allow them to pay a fraction of what the average worker contributes. Corporations argue that raising wages would "hurt the economy," ignoring the fact that their record profits come directly from underpaying their employees.

Even secular ethics aren't immune to the virus. In business schools and corporate seminars, greed is rebranded as "ambition" or "entrepreneurship." Students are taught that maximizing shareholder value is the ultimate goal, regardless of the human or environmental cost. This isn't just a perversion of morality, it's a complete erasure of it. By turning greed into a virtue, the virus ensures that its hosts feel no guilt or responsibility for the harm they cause.

Environmental Collapse: The Planet as Collateral Damage

Perhaps the most catastrophic consequence of the Greed Virus is its impact on the planet. The relentless pursuit of profit has turned the Earth into a resource to be extracted, exploited, and discarded. From deforestation to climate change, the virus treats environmental destruction as just another cost of doing business.

Consider the fossil fuel industry, one of the most obvious examples of greed-driven environmental harm. Oil companies like ExxonMobil and Chevron have known for decades that their activities contribute to climate change. Internal documents from the 1970s show that Exxon scientists accurately predicted rising global temperatures and sea levels due to carbon emissions. Did they change their practices? Of course not. Instead, they launched massive disinformation campaigns to sow doubt about climate science, ensuring that they could continue profiting from environmental destruction.

The Greed Virus doesn't stop with fossil fuels. It infects every industry that relies on natural resources. Deforestation in the Amazon, driven by agriculture and logging, is destroying one of the planet's most vital ecosystems. Overfishing is depleting ocean biodiversity at an alarming rate, threatening global food supplies. Even the tech industry, which markets itself as forward-thinking, relies on environmentally devastating practices. The mining of rare earth metals for smartphones and electric vehicles often involves child labor and the destruction of local environments in developing countries.

And what do the virus's hosts do about this destruction? They double down. Instead of investing in sustainable practices, they greenwash their activities, launching **PR** campaigns that tout minor eco-friendly initiatives while continuing to pollute at scale. Billionaires like Jeff Bezos announce token environmental funds, donating a fraction of their wealth to climate causes while their companies remain major polluters. Governments, many of them infected by the virus, subsidize fossil fuels and agriculture that harm the planet instead of supporting renewable energy and conservation efforts.

The consequences of this greed-fueled destruction are becoming impossible to ignore. Wildfires, hurricanes, and droughts are increasing in frequency and intensity, displacing millions. Biodiversity is collapsing, with species going extinct at rates not seen since the last mass extinction event. And yet, the hosts of the Greed Virus continue to prioritize short-term profits over long-term survival, dooming the planet to a future of unimaginable suffering.

How the Greed Virus Infects Individuals

The Greed Virus doesn't just target systems, it infects individuals, reshaping how people think, act, and relate to one another. It replaces community with competition, empathy with self-interest, and purpose with profit. This psychological manipulation ensures that the virus's hosts aren't just billionaires and corporations, they're everyday people who have been conditioned to uphold the system.

Take the normalization of overwork. Infected by the virus, society glorifies the "hustle" mentality, where working long hours and sacrificing personal well-being are seen as badges of honor. This isn't a coincidence, it's a deliberate effort to keep people too busy and too tired to question the system. Employers exploit this mindset, demanding unpaid overtime

and promoting toxic productivity cultures that leave workers
burned out and disposable.

The virus also weaponizes fear. It convinces individuals that
their neighbors are competitors, that immigrants are threats,
and that there's never enough to go around. This scarcity
mindset keeps people divided, ensuring that they fight each
other for scraps instead of uniting to challenge the system. It's
why billionaires like Elon Musk spread anti-union propaganda
and why media outlets owned by the wealthy stoke racial and
cultural tensions. Division is a tool of the virus, keeping its hosts
in power by preventing collective action.

The Greed Virus has infected culture, morality, and the planet
itself, turning every aspect of life into a tool for exploitation. Its
hosts profit while society suffers, and its effects are so pervasive
that they often feel inevitable. But they're not. Recognizing the
virus is the first step toward curing it. The next is fighting back,
through collective action, systemic change, and a rejection of
the values the virus has imposed. It's time to reclaim culture,
rebuild morality, and prioritize the planet over profit. The fight
against the Greed Virus isn't just necessary, it's possible. And it
starts now.

~4
The Circus of Capitalism

The spectacle of capitalism is a grotesque circus, a never-ending performance where the wealthy and powerful sit atop gilded thrones, tossing scraps to the desperate crowds below. They call it a system of opportunity, of competition, of free markets where anyone willing to work hard enough can carve out a piece of prosperity. But that is the illusion, the well-rehearsed lie that keeps the masses entertained while their pockets are emptied, their labor exploited, their futures sold off to the highest bidder. The reality is that capitalism is not a fair game, it is a rigged performance, a grotesque sideshow where billionaires and corporate overlords set the rules, control the outcomes, and feast on the wreckage they leave behind.

Every tent in this circus is designed to extract wealth from the working class while feeding the insatiable greed of the ruling elite. The healthcare system is one of the biggest attractions, a dazzling funhouse where people are promised care and protection, only to find themselves trapped in a maze of debt, bureaucracy, and corporate profit schemes. Insurance companies act as carnival barkers, convincing people to hand over their money in exchange for the illusion of security, only to deny them coverage when they need it most. Pharmaceutical companies jack up prices on life-saving medications, turning desperate patients into profit streams, ensuring that sickness and suffering are not problems to be solved but markets to be exploited. Hospitals operate like casinos, where the house always wins, and a single accident, a single diagnosis, can cost a person everything they have ever worked for.

Education is another rigged game, a pay-to-play system where wealth determines access and opportunity. Public schools are deliberately underfunded, gutted in favor of privatization schemes that funnel taxpayer money into corporate-run charter schools. Higher education has become a debt trap, a predatory system where young people are told that a degree is the only path to success, only to graduate with crushing loans and no guarantees of stable employment. The billionaire class, having already secured their children's futures through private schools and elite universities, tell the working class to simply pull themselves up by their bootstraps, while ensuring that those very bootstraps are kept just out of reach. They have turned learning into a commodity, a privilege rather than a right, making sure that knowledge, and the power it brings, remains concentrated in their hands.

Housing, one of the most basic human needs, has been transformed into a high-stakes game of monopoly, where billionaires and hedge funds buy up entire neighborhoods, driving up rents, forcing out longtime residents, and turning homes into speculative assets. The circus of capitalism dictates that shelter is not a guarantee but a luxury, that a roof over one's head is something to be earned through submission to the system, through the endless grind of wage labor and debt. Homelessness is not an accident, it is a deliberate outcome, a mechanism of control that keeps people fearful, desperate, willing to accept any terms just to stay afloat. The politicians who claim to care about affordable housing take massive donations from real estate developers and landlords, ensuring that nothing ever truly changes, that the housing crisis remains an unsolvable problem because it is far too profitable to fix.

The labor market is the main attraction, a nightmarish house of mirrors where workers are told they are free while being shackled to jobs that exploit them, underpay them, and grind them into dust. The corporate overlords praise "hard work" and "dedication" while raking in record profits, slashing benefits, and automating jobs out of existence. They sell the lie of meritocracy while paying starvation wages, outsourcing labor to sweatshops, and gutting unions to ensure that workers remain powerless. They dress it up in patriotic rhetoric, telling people that capitalism is about choice, about the freedom to succeed, while ensuring that most people's choices boil down to which form of exploitation they can endure.

The circus thrives on distraction. It needs people to look away, to focus on manufactured culture wars, on petty divisions, on meaningless debates designed to pit the working class against itself while the ruling elite plunder the world. The politicians and corporate executives who benefit from this system do not want people questioning why wages have stagnated while CEO pay has skyrocketed. They do not want people asking why billionaires can hoard unimaginable wealth while children go hungry. They do not want people to realize that their suffering is not an unfortunate side effect of capitalism but its intended outcome. So, they fill the airwaves with noise, with scandals, with outrage cycles that lead nowhere. They create enemies, immigrants, the poor, the "woke left," anyone who can be blamed for the very problems they created, so that people never look up, never see the puppet masters pulling the strings.

And all the while, the perverts at the top expand their empire, consolidating wealth and power, turning every aspect of life into a revenue stream. They privatize public goods, gut social safety nets, and then tell people that government is the problem, that the only solution is more deregulation, more tax cuts, more concessions to the billionaire class. They break systems, declare them failures, and then sell off the pieces for profit. They turn water into a commodity, healthcare into an investment, education into a privilege, and then they have the audacity to call it freedom.

But this circus is not sustainable. The greed virus that fuels it is all-consuming, devouring resources, hollowing out societies, driving billions into poverty while a handful of grotesquely wealthy men hoard more than they could ever spend in a thousand lifetimes. The illusion is cracking. The audience is starting to see through the smoke and mirrors, to realize that they have been conned, exploited, trapped in a system designed to keep them struggling while a small handful feast. And that is why the billionaires and the fascists cling to power so desperately, because they know that if enough people wake up, if enough people stop playing along, the whole thing collapses.

This is the grotesque carnival of capitalism, a dystopian sideshow where suffering is monetized, where human lives are treated as expendable, where every crisis is another opportunity for profit. It is a rigged game, designed by and for the ruling class, sustained by the myths of hard work, competition, and freedom that mask the brutal reality of exploitation and control. And the only way out of this nightmare is to stop believing in the illusion, to recognize that the show does not have to go on, that the tents can be burned to the ground, that the clowns running the circus can be thrown into the cages they built for everyone else. Because this is not the only way the world can be. The circus only continues as long as people keep buying tickets. The moment they refuse, the moment they turn their backs, the whole thing comes crashing down.

The greatest trick of capitalism's grotesque circus is convincing people that this is the only possible way to organize society. From the moment people are born, they are conditioned to believe in the sacredness of the market, in the myth that competition breeds excellence, that hard work leads to prosperity, that freedom is defined by the ability to consume. Every institution reinforces these ideas. Schools do not teach students how to question capitalism, only how to participate in it. The media, owned by the very billionaires who profit from this system, flood the airwaves with stories about individual success, about the self-made millionaire who pulled themselves up by sheer willpower while conveniently ignoring the millions who toil in obscurity, struggling to make ends meet despite working harder than any billionaire ever has. Religion, too, is often bent into submission, twisted into a justification for greed, for suffering, for submission to the so-called natural order where the rich are exalted as chosen by God and the poor are told their suffering will be rewarded in another life.

But reality tells a different story. The so-called free market is a lie, a carefully managed system where those at the top write the rules to ensure they never lose. Competition is a joke, massive corporations devour small businesses, consolidate industries, and then turn around and claim they are simply winning the game of capitalism. The very people who champion "free enterprise" and "small government" are the first to demand bailouts when their reckless speculation collapses the economy. They are the first to lobby for special tax breaks, for subsidies, for government contracts that funnel public money into their pockets. The market is not free, it is rigged, manipulated, controlled by a handful of corporate overlords who ensure that wealth flows only in one direction: up.

And while the ruling class hoards unimaginable wealth, the rest of society is forced into an endless struggle for survival. Wages remain stagnant while the cost of living skyrockets. Healthcare, housing, education, things that should be guaranteed as basic human rights, are transformed into high-priced commodities, luxuries accessible only to those who can afford them. People are told to work harder, to take on multiple jobs, to sacrifice their health and happiness, all while being shamed for not "managing their money properly." The billionaire class insists that poverty is a personal failing rather than the result of an economic system designed to extract wealth from the bottom and funnel it to the top. And when the pressure becomes too great, when people crack under the weight of financial stress, of endless labor with no reward, capitalism has a solution for that, too, pay for therapy, pay for medication, pay to escape the very system that is crushing you.

The circus thrives on crises. Every disaster, whether economic, environmental, or medical, is another opportunity to extract wealth. When the housing market collapsed in 2008, millions of people lost their homes, their savings, their futures. And what did the government do? It bailed out the banks, handed billions of dollars to the very institutions that had created the crisis, while ordinary people were left to rot. During the pandemic, while essential workers were risking their lives, while families were grieving, billionaires were getting richer. They raised prices, slashed wages, and profited off of death while the world burned. And when people began to demand better wages, better working conditions, the circus barkers of capitalism screamed about "lazy workers" and "labor shortages," pretending that the problem was people demanding too much rather than corporations refusing to pay fair wages.

And yet, despite all this, despite the overwhelming evidence that this system is nothing more than organized theft, the ruling class continues to sell capitalism as a meritocracy. They prop up the rare success stories, the single mother who became a millionaire, the immigrant who built a tech empire, while ignoring the millions who never escape the poverty they were born into. They rely on these outliers to maintain the illusion that success is within reach for anyone willing to work for it, even though the numbers tell a different story. The majority of wealth is inherited, not earned. Social mobility is a myth, most people die in the same economic class they were born into.

The final trick of capitalism's circus is convincing people that they are powerless to change it. The billionaires who own the economy, the politicians who protect their interests, the media that shapes public opinion, they all work together to reinforce the idea that this system is too big to dismantle, too complex to fix, too entrenched to overthrow. They ensure that people remain distracted, exhausted, divided. They pit workers against each other, stir up cultural wars, manufacture outrage over meaningless issues so that no one focuses on the real enemy. They tell people that the only way to change the system is through incremental reforms, through working within the very system that is designed to keep them powerless.

But history proves otherwise. No ruling class has ever relinquished power willingly. No exploitative system has ever been reformed into justice. The only way to end this nightmare is to destroy the circus entirely, to tear down the structures that uphold capitalist exploitation and replace them with something better. That means rejecting the myth that billionaires should exist and refusing to accept that housing, healthcare, and education should be for sale. The ruling class fears one thing above all: the people realizing their own power. They fear what happens when workers refuse to be exploited, when communities reclaim their resources, when the illusion of meritocracy shatters. They fear what happens when the audience stops watching, stops buying tickets to their circus, stops believing in their lies. Without that obedience, the entire system collapses. The tents fall, the lights go out, and the billionaires who once ran the show are left with nothing but the wreckage of their stolen empire.

Capitalism is not an unchangeable force, it is a man-made system, and what has been built can be torn down. The circus does not have to go on. The moment people refuse to play along, to walk away from the illusion, to build something new, the show ends. And when that day comes, when the last billionaire is stripped of their stolen wealth, there will be no nostalgia for the old world. No longing for the spectacle, the deception, the lies. There will only be the long-overdue realization that the world was always meant to be ours. And the future, finally, will belong to the many, not the few.

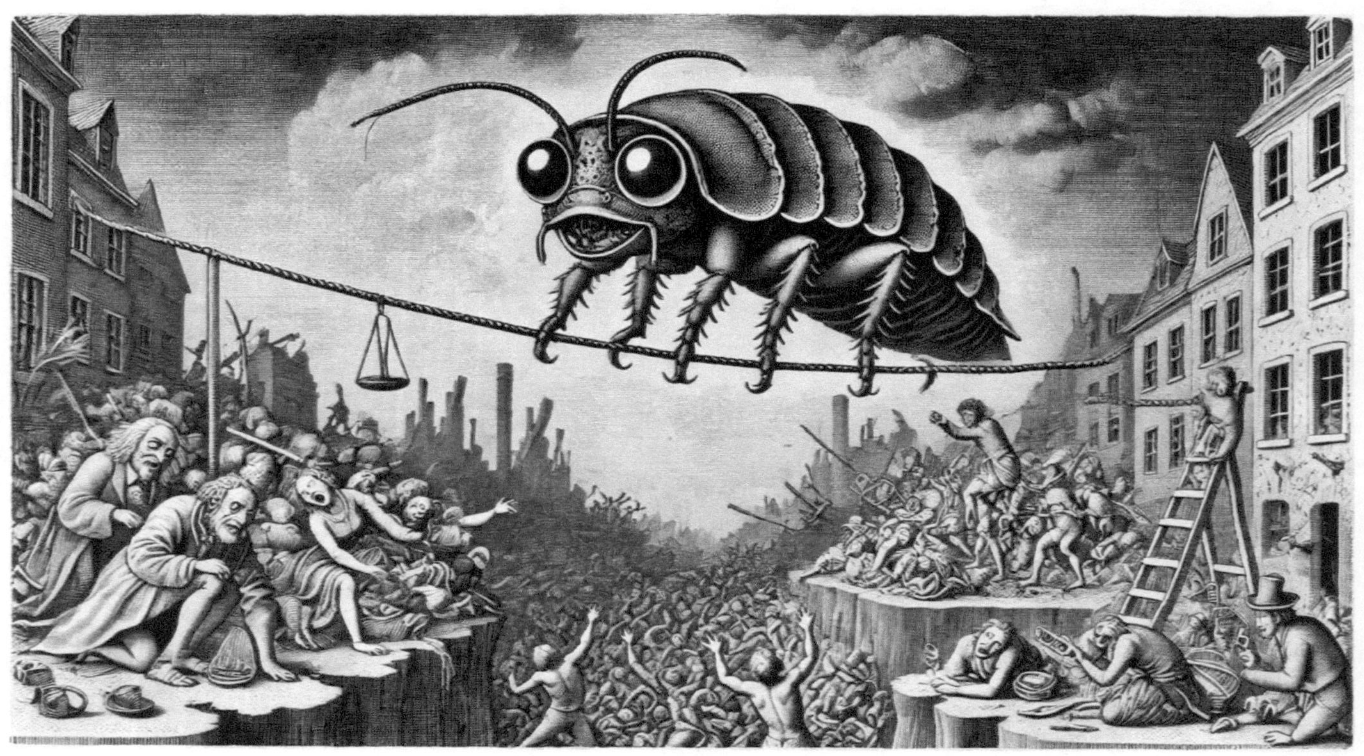

~5
The Pervert Show of Inequality

The perverts of power have always thrived on inequality. It is not a flaw in their system; it is the system. They need it, nurture it, and fortify it at every turn because their wealth and influence depend on keeping others in a permanent state of struggle. They do not just allow suffering; they manufacture it, engineer it, refine it into a tool of control. And when people begin to question why they are drowning in debt, why they have no access to healthcare, why their wages have remained stagnant while corporate profits soar, the perverts drape themselves in the cloak of morality and call it *family values*. They sell the myth that suffering is righteous, that economic hardship builds character, that the real threat to stability is not the billionaires hoarding wealth but the marginalized communities daring to demand dignity.

The pervert show of inequality is a grand performance, carefully scripted to keep people too exhausted, too overburdened, too beaten down to fight back. It is a spectacle where the villains masquerade as protectors of the moral order, all while ensuring that the people beneath them never have enough resources to challenge their authority. Every law they pass, every system they uphold, every justification they spew is designed to deepen inequality and tighten their grip on power. They are not just indifferent to suffering, they revel in it.

Look no further than the way they dismantle protections for victims of domestic abuse. They cry about the sanctity of marriage while gutting laws that protect women from violent spouses. They slash funding for shelters, roll back restraining order enforcement, and push for "fathers' rights" legislation that traps women and children in abusive situations. In the states where they have the most control, they enact policies that make it nearly impossible for victims to escape, forcing them into poverty and dependence. Then, they turn around and claim that single mothers are the real problem, that women who leave their abusers are breaking apart the family unit. They do not care about protecting families, they care about protecting abusers. Because the perverts who write these laws, who fund these movements, who sit in government office, have far more in common with the violent men they shield than with the victims they condemn.

And when they are not actively making life more dangerous for women, they are exploiting people of color for cheap labor. They criminalize poverty, transforming the prison system into a modern-day slave trade. They strip workers of protections, ensuring that undocumented immigrants and marginalized communities are forced into backbreaking jobs with no legal recourse against mistreatment. They demonize unions, push for "right to work" laws, and ship jobs overseas to places where labor laws are even weaker, all while blaming immigrants for taking jobs that were never going to be offered to American workers in the first place. And when those workers dare to demand fair pay or humane conditions, they unleash law enforcement to crush dissent, turning peaceful protests into battlegrounds, all in service of maintaining their exploitative status quo.

Their entire system is built on denying basic human rights while wrapping themselves in the rhetoric of morality and faith. They claim to be champions of life, but they let children starve. They claim to support families, but they strip away maternity leave, universal childcare, and affordable healthcare. They talk about law and order, but they protect rapists, abusers, and corrupt politicians while punishing the poor for being poor. They have built a world where survival is contingent upon
60

submission, where the cost of living keeps rising while wages
stay frozen, where education is a privilege, not a right, where
debt is the modern form of servitude, chaining entire
generations to a lifetime of economic despair.

And yet, they have convinced millions to worship this system,
to defend it, to believe that this is the natural order of things.
They sell the lie that anyone can make it if they just work hard
enough, despite the fact that the playing field has never been
level. They manipulate religion to reinforce the idea that
suffering is a test, that the poor are being refined in the fire of
struggle while the rich are simply reaping the rewards of their
righteousness. They manufacture consent for their cruelty by
turning faith into a weapon, making inequality seem not just
acceptable but *holy*.

But what is *holy* about a system that forces people to choose
between paying rent and buying food? What is *righteous* about
protecting corporations that exploit workers while punishing
the workers for demanding dignity? What is *just* about turning
away from the suffering of the most vulnerable while
billionaires set up tax shelters and offshore accounts to hoard
more than they could spend in a thousand lifetimes?

The truth is, the perverts in power do not care about morality.
They do not care about family, faith, community, or decency.
They only care about maintaining their own dominance, and
they will use every tool at their disposal, economic oppression,
religious dogma, cultural manipulation, to ensure that they are
never held accountable. They will continue gutting protections
for the vulnerable, exploiting workers, and concentrating
wealth at the top, all while demanding that the people they
oppress remain grateful for whatever scraps they are allowed to
keep.

And the worst part? They have spent so long getting away with
it that they truly believe they will never be stopped. They
believe that inequality is their right, that suffering is inevitable,

that people will never rise against them because they have built a machine so effective, so insidious, that even those who are crushed beneath it have been conditioned to defend it. They believe they can continue stripping away rights, hoarding resources, and using faith as a shield without consequence. The perverts in power may think they have secured their rule indefinitely, but they are mistaken. The illusion is cracking, the lies unraveling. And when enough people refuse to play their game, refuse to be manipulated, refuse to accept a world where suffering is profitable, the entire structure will collapse.

Their power is not invincible. Their wealth does not make them gods. When the people they have exploited, abused, and oppressed for generations finally turn against them, there will be no salvation for the perverts of inequality. Only justice.

The perverts who run this show do not just rely on inequality to maintain power; they actively expand it, ensuring that the divide between the wealthy and the working class, between the powerful and the powerless, is never bridged. It is not enough for them to be rich, they must ensure that others are poor. They strip communities of resources, gut social programs, and then blame the very people they have impoverished for their own suffering. It is a cycle of manufactured misery, a system so perfectly engineered that those trapped within it often cannot even see the strings being pulled above them.

These are the same people who, for decades, have fought against every attempt to raise the minimum wage, arguing that even a modest increase would somehow destroy the economy. Meanwhile, their own wealth skyrockets. CEO salaries have ballooned to obscene levels, stock buybacks funnel profits into the pockets of the already wealthy, and corporations boast about record earnings while claiming they cannot afford to pay workers a living wage. If a worker fights for better pay, they are fired. If a union tries to form, it is crushed. If an industry becomes too empowered, it is outsourced, automated, or deregulated into submission.

But this is not just about economic oppression. The perverts of inequality know that controlling wealth is only part of the equation, they must also control culture, history, and information. This is why they rewrite history, ban books, and attack education itself. They do not want people learning about past revolutions, about workers' rights movements, about the systemic theft of wealth and labor that built the very empires they now rule. They weaponize ignorance, ensuring that schools teach obedience rather than critical thinking, that media reinforces consumerism rather than solidarity, that people grow up internalizing the idea that suffering is just how the world works rather than something that has been forced upon them.

They have perfected the art of manipulating public outrage to distract from their crimes. They funnel billions into manufactured culture wars, keeping the masses focused on petty divisions while they loot the planet. They tell working-class white Americans that immigrants are stealing their jobs while the real culprits, the corporate overlords and billionaire class, hoard wealth at unprecedented levels. They tell men that feminism is their enemy while quietly dismantling labor protections, ensuring that both men and women are working longer hours for less pay. They push religious extremism, demonizing LGBTQ people, attacking reproductive rights, and manufacturing moral panics around classrooms and bathrooms, all while quietly stealing trillions from public funds and locking in policies that will make future generations even more powerless. They pit people against each other, by race, by gender, by nationality, because as long as the working class is divided, they will never turn their rage toward the people truly responsible for their suffering.

And when all else fails, they use fear. Fear of crime, fear of instability, fear of the unknown. They manufacture crises, allowing infrastructure to crumble, allowing housing to become unaffordable, allowing healthcare to become a privilege rather than a right. They let people teeter on the edge of desperation so that when the ruling class offers them a scapegoat, a migrant, a protester, a "woke" politician, many will jump at the chance to blame someone, anyone, other than the billionaires and corporate monopolies running the entire system into the ground.

This grotesque spectacle is not limited to the economy, to wages, to labor exploitation, it extends into every aspect of life, particularly into the way society treats women and marginalized communities. They have worked tirelessly to strip away reproductive rights, forcing women into a position of economic and physical dependence. They gut protections against domestic violence while insisting that the real crisis is women being "too independent." They roll back child labor laws, ensuring that poor families are forced to send their children into the workforce just to survive. They criminalize pregnancy outcomes, turning miscarriages into potential death sentences for women who cannot prove their innocence. They preach about family values while making it harder for families to survive. The hypocrisy is staggering, but it is not accidental, it is a necessary function of their power.

And when it comes to the treatment of people of color, the cruelty becomes even more blatant. Prisons are filled with Black and brown bodies, arrested for minor infractions while white-collar criminals steal billions and walk free. The police, who exist to protect property rather than people, unleash military-grade force on peaceful protesters while turning a blind eye to corporate crime. Environmental racism ensures that the poorest communities, often communities of color, are poisoned, displaced, and stripped of resources. The billionaires who create these crises then turn around and offer charity, laundering their reputations while the people they harmed remain trapped in poverty and despair.

This is the pervert show of inequality. It is a system where suffering is profitable, where exploitation is enshrined as law, where billionaires pose as benevolent overlords while draining entire nations of their resources. It is a system where human lives are mere commodities, where basic rights are stripped away under the guise of morality, where the people responsible for the worst crimes are the ones writing the laws that keep them in power.

The cracks in the illusion are already beginning to show. People are waking up, recognizing the patterns, rejecting the lies. Workers are organizing, renters are demanding justice, young people are refusing to accept a future dictated by greed. The ruling class is terrified, which is why they are doubling down, stripping away rights faster than ever, criminalizing protest, and normalizing dystopia. They know that if people recognize the truth, that inequality is not inevitable, that capitalism is not the only option, that the world can be built differently, their power is finished.

But recognition alone is not enough. The people who suffer under this system must be willing to fight. They must reject the false morality that justifies suffering. They must refuse to be distracted by manufactured culture wars. They must understand that true power lies in collective action, in solidarity, in the refusal to comply with a system built to exploit them. The pervert show of inequality only continues as long as people play along. The moment enough people refuse, the show ends. And when it does, those who profited from generations of suffering will finally face the consequences of their greed.

~6
Billionaire Clowns: Laughing to the Bank

The billionaire class is not just an economic force, it is a grotesque spectacle, a circus of greed where the wealthiest people on the planet play sadistic games with the lives of millions. They hoard wealth at unimaginable levels, amassing fortunes so vast that they could single-handedly end world hunger, provide universal healthcare, or rebuild entire nations. But they do none of that. Instead, they treat the world as their private casino, where the chips are human lives, and the bets are placed on which industry they can extract, exploit, and destroy next. These billionaires laugh all the way to the bank while the rest of society is left gasping for air, drowning under rising costs, shrinking wages, and an ever-expanding gap between the haves and have-nots.

These modern-day robber barons don't just profit from destruction, they revel in it. They sit atop their obscene fortunes, jetting between luxury compounds while entire communities collapse under the weight of their greed. They push policies that strip workers of rights, gut environmental protections, and slash taxes for themselves while ensuring that ordinary people pay more for less. They break governments, then buy them out. They gut public infrastructure, then sell it back at a premium. They engineer recessions, then swoop in to buy foreclosed homes for pennies on the dollar. Every crisis is an opportunity, every disaster a payday, every act of mass suffering just another number on their ever-growing profit margins. They are not just indifferent to human suffering, they thrive on it. Their wealth depends on keeping people poor, desperate, and afraid.

Yet, despite their flagrant abuses, billionaires are not demonized. They are deified. They are held up as geniuses, job creators, visionaries, the apex of human achievement. The media fawns over them, chronicling their extravagant lifestyles, their expensive hobbies, their whims and eccentricities as though they are the stuff of legends rather than symptoms of a deeply diseased economic system. Instead of being scrutinized, they are worshipped. Instead of being taxed, they are given more loopholes to hide their wealth. And when they inevitably crash the economy, whether through reckless speculation, corporate fraud, or outright theft, the government steps in not to punish them, but to bail them out, ensuring that they remain insulated from the consequences of their own greed while the rest of society foots the bill.

And make no mistake, billionaires are not simply rich people who got lucky. They are an elite class that exists solely because of systemic theft. No one "earns" a billion dollars. It is impossible to ethically amass that much wealth. Billionaires accumulate their fortunes by exploiting labor, extracting resources, and rigging financial systems to ensure that wealth flows ever-upward. They do not create jobs, they create wage slavery. They do not innovate, hey buy patents, monopolize industries, and block competitors from emerging. They do not improve society, they privatize it, ensuring that every aspect of life, from healthcare to education to basic survival, comes with a price tag that guarantees their continued profit. Their entire existence is a testament to the fact that capitalism is not about merit, it is about power.

Nowhere is this more evident than in the way billionaires treat the environment. These clowns, who claim to be visionaries, are in reality the architects of climate destruction. They have known for decades that their industries, fossil fuels, manufacturing, industrial agriculture, are rapidly accelerating climate collapse. They have had the data, the science, the warnings. And what have they done? They have doubled down. They have poured billions into disinformation campaigns, hired lobbyists to gut environmental regulations, and funded politicians who deny climate change while their own private scientists confirm it. They are not ignorant of the destruction they are causing. They are fully aware. They just do not care.

When the wildfires rage, when the hurricanes intensify, when the heatwaves turn cities into ovens, billionaires are nowhere to be found. They are in their bunkers, in their climate-controlled mansions, on their yachts far from the chaos they created. They are hoarding land in New Zealand, buying up water rights, preparing their escape routes while the rest of humanity is left to suffer the consequences of their greed. And the worst part? They have the audacity to tell the rest of us to recycle, to turn off our lights, to carpool, small, insignificant actions that pale in comparison to the environmental devastation they unleash every single day. The top 1% of the world's richest individuals are responsible for more carbon emissions than the poorest half of the planet combined. Yet they continue to act as if the burden of fixing the planet falls on ordinary people while they hoard wealth and resources with no accountability.

But their greed is not just economic and environmental, it is also deeply political. Billionaires are not content to merely own industries. They want to own entire governments. They fund campaigns, buy politicians, and manipulate elections to ensure that no policies are ever passed that could threaten their power. They do not just lobby, they write the laws themselves. They are the reason tax rates for the rich keep dropping. They are the reason healthcare remains privatized and unaffordable. They are the reason labor protections continue to erode while corporate profits skyrocket. They own the system because they designed the system.

Perhaps the most grotesque perversion of their power, however, is the way they have wrapped themselves in religion. More and more billionaires are positioning themselves as "ordained by God," using faith as both a shield and a weapon. They fund mega-churches, Christian nationalist movements, and right-wing religious institutions, all while claiming that their obscene wealth is a sign of divine favor rather than the result of theft and exploitation. This is not new, throughout history, tyrants and oligarchs have always used religion to justify their rule, but in the modern era, it has reached new heights of absurdity. These men, who exploit workers, dodge taxes, hoard resources, and fund endless wars, now claim to be humble servants of God. They use biblical language to defend capitalism, twisting scripture to imply that poverty is a sign of moral failing while wealth is a reward for righteousness. They promote the prosperity gospel, a grotesque ideology that tells struggling people to pray for riches while the rich get richer through systemic looting.

This fusion of billionaire greed and religious extremism is perhaps the most dangerous element of their rule. It ensures that they are not just seen as wealthy men, they are seen as chosen men. They are not just businessmen, they are prophets, messiahs, anointed leaders whose wealth is proof of their divine favor. And because they have wrapped their economic exploitation in religious rhetoric, they make it nearly impossible for many to question their power. To resist them is to resist God. To tax them is to defy His plan. To challenge their authority is to attack not just the ruling class, but the very fabric of faith itself.

This is the real billionaire circus, a show where the clowns are not funny but terrifying, where the ringmasters are not entertainers but oligarchs, and where the audience is not laughing but suffering. These billionaires are not just hoarding wealth, they are hoarding the future itself. They have stolen resources, dismantled democracies, gutted the planet, and still, they demand more. They will never stop unless they are made

70

to stop. They will never relinquish their power unless it is taken from them. And they will never, ever act in the interest of humanity because their entire existence is proof that the only thing they worship, the only thing they truly believe in, is themselves.

This is the world they have built, and they expect the rest of us to live in it, to suffer under it, to accept it as normal. But it is not normal. It is a grotesque distortion of what is possible. The billionaire circus is not inevitable. It is a con. And once enough people realize that, the tent collapses, the stage crumbles, and the clowns, for the first time, will have no one left to laugh with them.

The billionaire class doesn't just accumulate wealth, they hoard it like a sickness, stuffing their bank accounts with numbers so large they cease to have any real meaning, all while millions of people struggle to afford basic necessities. They have built a world where starvation exists next to food waste, where homelessness flourishes while luxury apartments sit empty, where medicine is stockpiled by corporations while sick children are turned away at hospital doors. This is not just inequality. This is a deliberately constructed system of greed, designed to ensure that wealth never stops flowing upward, that power remains concentrated in the hands of a few, and that the rest of humanity is locked in a perpetual state of precarity. The billionaire class thrives not in spite of human suffering, but because of it. Every moment of desperation, every instance of struggle, every financial collapse, every war, every crisis, it all feeds their machine.

Take, for instance, the housing market, one of the most blatant examples of billionaire greed in action. Decades ago, a home was something a working-class family could afford on a single income. Now, thanks to speculative real estate investment by hedge funds and billionaire-backed corporations, homeownership is a fantasy for an entire generation. Rent has skyrocketed, wages have stagnated, and evictions are at an all-time high. BlackRock, Vanguard, and other financial giants are gobbling up single-family homes by the thousands, turning what was once a fundamental human right, shelter, into just another asset on their balance sheets. They don't just own property; they own the right to dictate who gets to live where and under what conditions. They have ensured that housing insecurity is the norm, that people are so burdened with rent and debt that they have no time or energy left to fight back against the system that is suffocating them.

And it isn't just housing. The same playbook is being used in every sector, from healthcare to food production to education. Corporations, backed by billionaire investors, have taken over industries that were once about meeting human needs and turned them into profit extraction machines. Hospitals are run by private equity firms that slash staff and deny care to boost earnings. Grocery chains manipulate food prices, driving up costs for consumers while raking in record profits. Universities operate like businesses, drowning students in debt while paying administrators multimillion-dollar salaries. The billionaire class is not content with merely profiting off goods and services, they profit off survival itself. They control the conditions under which people live and die, and they do so with the full knowledge that their actions are causing irreversible harm.

And when the consequences of their greed become too obvious to ignore, what do they do? They lie. They spin narratives designed to convince people that the system is working exactly as it should, that their suffering is either their own fault or an unfortunate side effect of progress. They fund think tanks that churn out propaganda about the virtues of free markets while quietly ensuring that those markets are anything but free. They bankroll politicians who strip away social safety nets and then claim the resulting misery is simply the natural order of things. They manipulate public discourse, controlling the flow of information through media outlets they own, ensuring that the conversation around wealth and power is always tilted in their favor.

But perhaps the greatest trick of the billionaire class is their ability to manufacture distraction. They understand that if people were to truly focus on economic injustice, on the grotesque disparities in wealth and power, there would be a revolution. So they create chaos. They fund culture wars, stoking division between racial groups, between men and women, between rural and urban communities, between the working class and the poor. They flood the airwaves with nonsense, ensuring that people are always arguing about something trivial rather than focusing on the real enemy. They frame taxation as theft, regulation as oppression, and wealth redistribution as communism, all while quietly siphoning more and more resources into their own pockets. They make sure that people are always fighting among themselves, too exhausted, too distracted, and too demoralized to challenge the system that keeps them trapped.

And when distraction doesn't work, they fall back on brute force. The billionaire class does not just control wealth, they control the mechanisms of state power. When workers try to unionize, billionaires send in the cops. When activists fight for environmental protections, billionaires fund politicians who criminalize protest. When movements for economic justice gain traction, billionaires unleash their media machines to smear them, to co-opt them, to turn them against themselves. They know that the moment people begin to see through their illusions, the entire facade of their power crumbles.

This is why they invest so heavily in political influence. Every election cycle, billions of dollars are funneled into campaigns, Super PACs, and dark money operations, ensuring that only candidates who serve the interests of the wealthy ever make it onto the ballot. The system is rigged from the start. Voter suppression, gerrymandering, and outright corruption ensure that policies benefiting the people never make it to the legislative floor. The billionaire class has made sure that democracy itself is little more than a spectacle, a performance designed to give the illusion of choice while keeping power firmly in the hands of those who already have it.

And yet, even with all their wealth, all their power, all their control, the billionaire class is terrified. They know that their system is unsustainable, that it is built on an illusion that is beginning to crack. They see the strikes, the protests, the growing discontent. They know that people are waking up to the con, that the myths of meritocracy and hard work are no longer enough to keep the masses docile. This is why they are ramping up their efforts to suppress opposition. They are expanding surveillance, criminalizing dissent, militarizing the police, and tightening their grip on the economy. They are preparing for a world in which they will have to fight to keep what they have stolen.

But here's the truth they don't want anyone to realize: they are vastly outnumbered. There are only a few thousand billionaires in the world, but there are billions of people struggling under their rule. If the working class, the poor, the disenfranchised ever unite, if they ever refuse to participate in the system that exploits them, if they ever decide that the billionaire class is not just unnecessary but actively harmful, the entire structure collapses. The billionaires are not untouchable. They are not gods. They are not invincible. They are parasites, clinging to a system that only functions because people allow it to.

The billionaire circus does not have to continue. The world does not have to be dictated by the whims of a handful of sociopaths who see human life as just another asset to be traded. The tents can come down, the lights can go out, and the clowns can be thrown out of the ring. But that will only happen if people stop believing in the illusion, if they refuse to keep playing along, if they decide that they are not mere spectators in a world controlled by the wealthy but active participants in shaping something new.

And that is the greatest fear of the billionaire class, that people will stop seeing them as untouchable, that they will stop believing the lie that this is the only way the world can function. Because the moment that happens, the circus is over. And for the first time in generations, the people will take center stage.

~7
Divide and Infect

Fascism has never needed truth to thrive. It survives on spectacle, manipulation, and an unrelenting ability to pit people against one another. It is not just a political ideology; it is a strategy, a playbook perfected over generations. The fascists of today are not jackbooted soldiers marching through the streets in perfect formation, they are billionaires funding think tanks, media moguls crafting propaganda, politicians delivering dog whistles dressed up as policy proposals. They do not conquer by force alone. They conquer by division, by turning neighbor against neighbor, by convincing the oppressed to fight amongst themselves rather than against their real enemy. And at the heart of it all, fueling the entire machine, is the greed virus.

The greed virus is the ultimate weapon of fascism, not just because it consolidates wealth in the hands of the few, but because it ensures that the many are too busy fighting for scraps to challenge the system itself. The most effective way to prevent collective action is to make sure the people never see themselves as a collective. Divide and rule, it is one of the oldest tricks in the book. But in the modern era, it has become an art form. The ruling class knows that as long as workers are fighting over cultural issues, as long as people are consumed by manufactured outrage, as long as the poor are blaming each other instead of the rich, there will never be a serious challenge to their power.

This is why fascists use scapegoats. A system built on wealth hoarding and mass exploitation is always at risk of collapse, and the people in power know it. They know that sooner or later, the public will start looking for the source of their misery. So the fascists preemptively provide them with a target: immigrants, minorities, LGBTQ people, women, unions, protesters, activists, intellectuals, anyone who can be framed as an "other," as the reason for society's decline. They tell white working-class people that Black and brown communities are stealing their jobs while ensuring that wages are kept artificially low by corporate greed. They tell men that feminism has gone "too far" while gutting labor protections that would benefit all workers, regardless of gender. They tell Christians that they are under attack while using religious institutions as a means of funneling wealth into the hands of the powerful. They fabricate crises, about crime, about "woke" culture, about non-existent threats, to ensure that the public's anger is always misdirected.

And when the economy inevitably falters, when the people begin to feel the full weight of inequality pressing down on them, the fascists unleash their media arms to do what they do best: manipulate, misinform, and distract. News outlets owned by billionaires frame economic struggles as the fault of immigrants rather than the fault of outsourcing and wage suppression. Social media algorithms, carefully engineered to amplify division, ensure that the loudest and most extreme voices dominate public discourse. Fascist politicians, funded by corporate interests, push narratives designed to convince people that their problems stem from the marginalized rather than the wealthy elite hoarding resources. Every crisis is an opportunity, an opportunity to fracture solidarity, to spread paranoia, to reinforce the idea that the world is a zero-sum game where only the strong survive.

This is not just about propaganda, it is about control. The goal is not simply to spread misinformation but to cultivate a public so disoriented, so angry, so consumed by fear and resentment that they are incapable of organizing against their true

78

oppressors. Fascism does not need people to love it. It only needs them to hate something else more. It thrives in environments where trust is broken, where communities are fragmented, where people are so overwhelmed by chaos that they become desperate for a strongman to restore order. The ruling class does not care if people believe in their lies, it only matters that they believe in nothing else.

Take, for instance, the manufactured war on education. Fascists understand that an informed public is a dangerous public, so they attack knowledge itself. They ban books, rewrite history, and defund public schools, ensuring that future generations grow up without the tools to question authority. They frame universities as "leftist indoctrination camps" while pouring billions into conservative think tanks that flood the media with their own version of reality. They replace facts with conspiracy theories, ensuring that the people most impacted by systemic failure are too consumed by paranoia to recognize who is actually responsible. They create an environment where truth itself is under attack, where expertise is dismissed as elitism, where the idea of objective reality becomes just another battleground in the culture war.

And then there is the war on workers. Fascists cannot allow labor solidarity to take root because organized labor is one of the few forces capable of standing up to corporate power. So they demonize unions, frame strikes as selfish, push right-to-work laws that strip workers of bargaining power. They pit workers against each other, ensuring that people are too busy resenting their neighbors to notice that their real enemies are sitting in corporate boardrooms, funneling wealth to the top while cutting wages and benefits. They tell white workers that Black workers are stealing their opportunities. They tell native-born citizens that immigrants are lowering wages, all while quietly backing policies that ensure corporations can exploit cheap labor. They ensure that people are so focused on fighting each other that they never look up long enough to see the billionaires laughing behind closed doors.

And when division alone is not enough, fascists resort to fear. They paint entire populations as threats, as existential dangers to the survival of the nation. They claim that immigrants are flooding across borders to replace "real" citizens. They claim that LGBTQ people are corrupting children. They claim that activists fighting for justice are actually criminals trying to destroy society. They create moral panics out of nothing, convincing people that they are under siege, that their way of life is being stolen, that the only way to survive is to turn to authoritarianism for protection. The more fear they spread, the more power they consolidate. The more people feel threatened, the more willing they are to trade freedom for security. And once that trade is made, once people accept that democracy is a luxury they can no longer afford, the fascists have won.

This is how the greed virus spreads, not just through economic theft, but through cultural and political manipulation. It is not enough for the ruling class to steal wealth; they must also steal agency, solidarity, and hope. They must ensure that the people they exploit never recognize their own power, that they never come together in collective action, that they remain trapped in an endless loop of distraction, division, and despair.

And this is why fascism, despite all its pretenses, is ultimately a fragile system. It requires constant deception, relentless propaganda, an ever-expanding list of scapegoats. It can never allow for moments of unity, because unity would shatter the illusion that the system is too big to change. It can never allow people to see the world clearly, because a clear vision of reality would make the game all too obvious. It can never allow for a pause, because the moment people stop fighting each other, they might start fighting back.

But history shows that no empire of lies lasts forever. No system built on division remains unchallenged. The greed virus, for all its power, is not an incurable disease, it is a manufactured sickness, one that can be undone the moment enough people recognize it for what it is. Fascism's greatest fear is an informed, united, and fearless public. And that fear is justified. Because the moment people stop believing in the illusion, the entire system crumbles. The lies collapse under their own weight. The distractions lose their power. And the rulers who built their empires on deception will find themselves exposed, vulnerable, and, for the first time, truly afraid.

Fear is the fuel that keeps the fascist machine running. The billionaires, theocrats, and political strongmen who benefit from this system know that a public consumed by terror is a public that will willingly surrender its rights, its freedoms, and even its own interests in the name of self-preservation. Fear allows them to manufacture enemies where none exist, to scapegoat the powerless, and to keep the people from realizing the true nature of their suffering. This is why every authoritarian movement, every fascist uprising, has relied on the same tactics: find a target, paint them as a threat, and convince the majority that only the strong hand of power can keep them safe.

Take the so-called "immigration crisis," a favorite tool of fascists and oligarchs alike. These people know that economic instability breeds discontent, and they also know that they are the ones responsible for that instability. They could pay workers fair wages, regulate industries to prevent corporate abuse, and invest in communities to ensure economic stability, but they won't. That would require giving up even a fraction of their obscene wealth. Instead, they create an enemy. They blame immigrants, flooding the media with images of caravans, with stories about "illegals" stealing jobs and straining resources, with fear-mongering about crime and cultural decay. This narrative is not just false, it is a deliberate deception, designed to redirect anger away from the ruling class and onto people who have no real power.

And it works. The billionaire class, through its control of media and political institutions, has successfully convinced millions of people that the source of their economic suffering is not corporate greed, not tax cuts for the ultra-wealthy, not the dismantling of labor protections, but poor migrants trying to escape war, climate disaster, and economic ruin (ruin often caused by the very same corporations and billionaires now pointing the finger at them). This is how fascism spreads. It thrives in economic desperation, using it to create resentment, to divide the working class, to keep people too distracted and angry to see the real enemy standing right in front of them.

The same strategy is used against every marginalized group. Look at the relentless attacks on LGBTQ people, particularly trans people, in recent years. Why would billionaires and politicians suddenly develop an obsession with what bathrooms people use, what medical care trans youth receive, or what gender someone identifies as? Do they care about these issues on a personal level? Of course not. But they care about power. They care about keeping the masses engaged in a never-ending culture war, because as long as people are debating the existence of trans people, they're not talking about wealth inequality, corporate corruption, or political manipulation. These attacks are not organic, they are well-funded, orchestrated, and calculated to create hysteria. Laws restricting trans healthcare, bans on books featuring LGBTQ characters, moral panics over drag performances, these are not the actions of a government genuinely concerned with public well-being. They are manufactured crises, created to keep people divided, to keep them distracted, to keep them afraid.

Religious extremism plays a critical role in all of this, serving as both a justification for oppression and a tool for control. Fascists know that in order to maintain power, they need not just political and economic dominance, but moral legitimacy. They need people to believe that their suffering is not just necessary, but righteous. They need a framework that justifies inequality, that makes oppression seem like a divine mandate rather than a man-made system of control. This is why they prop up religious nationalism, turning faith into a weapon against democracy. In the United States, Christian nationalism

82

has been hijacked by the billionaire class to serve as the moral backbone of the fascist project. It allows them to justify forced birth laws, attacks on LGBTQ rights, and the dismantling of secular governance under the guise of "protecting traditional values." It ensures that the people most impacted by economic and social injustice turn to the church for answers, rather than questioning the systems that put them in that position in the first place.

Christian nationalism does not just demand obedience, it demands submission. It tells people that poverty is a test of faith, that suffering is holy, that rebellion is sin. It preaches that those in power have been chosen by God, that questioning authority is a sign of moral weakness. It turns the victims of fascism into willing participants in their own oppression. And most importantly, it gives fascists a pretext for expanding their control. The same politicians who cut food assistance programs, gut public housing, and suppress wages are the ones who claim to be fighting for "family values." The same lawmakers who take donations from oil companies and deregulate industries poisoning the planet are the ones claiming that God gave them dominion over the earth. The same billionaires funding endless wars, breaking unions, and suppressing voting rights are the ones calling themselves defenders of Christian civilization.

And what happens to the people who refuse to fall in line? They are labeled enemies. Anyone who fights for justice, for equality, for a redistribution of power and resources is painted as a radical, a terrorist, a danger to society. Fascists cannot allow solidarity to take root, because solidarity is the antidote to their power. The moment people stop seeing each other as enemies, the moment they begin to unite across race, gender, nationality, and class, the entire structure of control starts to weaken. This is why every fascist regime, every authoritarian movement, has cracked down on labor unions, activist groups, and progressive movements. They cannot allow the masses to recognize their shared struggle, because if they do, the ruling class falls.

Look at history. Every fascist movement has used division as its primary weapon. The Nazis scapegoated Jews, communists, LGBTQ people, and the disabled. Mussolini turned Italians against labor unions and socialists. The apartheid regime in South Africa kept the Black majority divided through artificial ethnic classifications. In every case, the ruling elite used fear, propaganda, and brute force to keep the people from recognizing their true enemy. And in every case, those divisions were not natural, they were manufactured. Today, the same playbook is being used. Fascists rely on division because they know they are outnumbered. They know that if the people ever stop fighting each other and start fighting back, their reign is over.

But history also teaches another lesson: unity is more powerful than fear. The civil rights movement, the labor movement, the anti-colonial struggles of the 20th century, all of them succeeded because people recognized that their fight was interconnected. The moment workers, marginalized groups, and the oppressed refuse to be divided, the fascist structure begins to crumble. This is why solidarity is the ultimate act of resistance. It is why every attempt at division must be met with radical, unwavering unity. It is why the greatest fear of every fascist is not a single political opponent, not a single law or policy, it is the people, standing together, refusing to be manipulated, refusing to be distracted, refusing to be afraid.

The greed virus has infected every level of society, but it is not an incurable disease. It spreads through fear and division, but it can be eradicated through awareness and resistance. The first step is recognizing the game being played, seeing through the lies, refusing to participate in the divisions that benefit the ruling class. The second step is action, organizing, educating, dismantling the systems that perpetuate inequality and oppression. Fascism cannot survive in a world where the people refuse to be divided. It cannot thrive in a society where workers see their struggles as interconnected, where people understand that their suffering is manufactured, where the myth of scarcity is replaced with the reality of abundance.

And most importantly, fascism cannot win if people refuse to give in to fear. Fear is its greatest weapon, but it is also its greatest weakness. Because once people stop fearing each other, once they stop fearing change, once they stop fearing their own power, the entire system falls apart. The ruling class will do everything in its power to keep people fighting amongst themselves, to keep them distracted, to keep them afraid. But if the people choose unity over division, courage over compliance, solidarity over scapegoating, then fascism has no future. The billionaires, the theocrats, the politicians clinging to power, they will find themselves facing an opponent they cannot defeat: the people, united, relentless, and ready to tear down the system that kept them in chains.

~8
The Christian Nationalist Shield

Christian nationalism in the United States has never been about faith, morality, or righteousness. It has always been about power. It is not a belief system; it is a political weapon, wielded by the ruling class to justify systemic oppression, economic exploitation, and social control. It is the perfect disguise for authoritarianism, allowing the most sadistic, wealth-obsessed perverts in power to masquerade as defenders of tradition, family, and morality while they strip away the rights of women, crush workers, and elevate white supremacy as divine law. Christian nationalism is not Christianity, it is a perversion of faith, carefully designed to serve the interests of the ruling elite while keeping the masses obedient, divided, and too afraid to question authority.

The people pushing this ideology are not true believers in any meaningful sense. They do not live according to the teachings of Christ, nor do they care about the values they claim to uphold. Their actions betray them at every turn. These are the same men who scream about "family values" while elevating serial sexual abusers to the highest offices of power. The same men who call themselves "pro-life" while slashing food assistance, blocking maternal healthcare, and ignoring the suffering of actual living, breathing children. The same men who claim to follow a humble, self-sacrificing savior while hoarding obscene amounts of wealth and demanding that the poor suffer in silence. This is not a religious movement. It is a racket, a con, a political strategy designed to justify cruelty while silencing opposition.

At its core, Christian nationalism is about enforcing a rigid, patriarchal, white supremacist order. It is about controlling women and girls, dictating what they can do with their bodies, their futures, and their lives. It is about criminalizing dissent, banning books, restricting education, and ensuring that the people most harmed by their policies remain too powerless to fight back. It is about upholding a system where wealth remains concentrated in the hands of a few, where billionaires are worshiped as "ordained by God," and where suffering is framed as a moral necessity rather than a direct consequence of deliberate policy choices.

Nowhere is this weaponization of faith more grotesque than in the forced birth movement. The people behind these policies are not interested in protecting life, they are interested in punishing women. They see pregnancy as a consequence, a form of social control, a way to ensure that women remain dependent, vulnerable, and unable to challenge the existing order. They know exactly what their laws will do. They know that banning abortion will lead to maternal deaths, that it will force children to carry pregnancies to term, that it will strip survivors of rape and incest of any agency over their own bodies. They know, and they do it anyway. Because cruelty is not a flaw in their system, it is the point.

Look at how they frame their laws. They do not just ban abortion; they criminalize it, turning doctors into criminals, forcing hospitals to deny life-saving care, making it impossible for women to seek medical help without fear of prosecution. They pass bounty-hunting laws that incentivize neighbors to spy on each other, encouraging the kind of state-sanctioned paranoia that turns communities against themselves. They push for "fetal personhood" laws that lay the groundwork for criminalizing miscarriage, ensuring that any woman who loses a pregnancy can be investigated and charged. They claim that these policies are about protecting the unborn, but their complete indifference to the suffering of women and children tells the real story. This is not about life. It is about control.

Christian nationalists are not content with simply restricting abortion; they want to roll back every gain women have made in the past century. They want to ban contraception, restrict women's ability to work and live independently, and redefine marriage as a tool of subjugation. They openly pine for an era when women had no legal rights, when they were treated as property, when their only role in society was to serve as wives, mothers, and breeders. And they are getting bolder in their ambitions. They do not just want to ban abortion in red states, they want a national ban. They do not just want to restrict reproductive rights, they want to criminalize any form of bodily autonomy that challenges their worldview.

And it is not just about women. Christian nationalism is also a weapon for enforcing white supremacy. It is no coincidence that the same people pushing forced birth laws are also attacking voting rights, demonizing immigrants, and trying to rewrite history to erase the realities of slavery, genocide, and segregation. The forced birth movement is directly tied to their broader goal of demographic control, ensuring that white Christian families remain the dominant force in American society. They frame their policies as a defense of tradition, but what they are really defending is a system of racial and gender hierarchy that benefits them at the expense of everyone else.

This is why they attack public education, banning any curriculum that challenges their revisionist history. This is why they push for book bans, targeting works that address racism, sexism, LGBTQ rights, and the realities of American imperialism. This is why they insist that America was founded as a Christian nation, despite overwhelming historical evidence to the contrary. Their goal is not just to legislate morality but to rewrite reality itself, to create a world where their narrow, oppressive version of history is the only one allowed to exist.

And as always, the hypocrisy is staggering. The same people who claim to be protecting religious freedom are the first to attack anyone who does not conform to their beliefs. They scream about "religious liberty" when it comes to denying healthcare, refusing service to LGBTQ people, or pushing Christianity into public schools, but they are silent when Muslims, Jews, or atheists demand the same protections. Their version of religious freedom is nothing more than a license to oppress, a free pass to force their ideology onto everyone else while shielding themselves from accountability.

Christian nationalism thrives on fear, and its leaders know that their power depends on keeping the masses afraid. They use the language of faith to justify authoritarianism, framing their policies as divine mandates rather than the calculated power grabs that they are. They claim that their war on reproductive rights is about saving babies, that their attacks on LGBTQ people are about protecting children, that their efforts to dismantle public institutions are about restoring morality. But it is all a lie. Their agenda is not moral. It is not righteous. It is not about faith. It is about control.

The rise of Christian nationalism in America is not an accident. It is a carefully orchestrated movement, backed by billionaires, corporate interests, and political operatives who see religion as the perfect vehicle for maintaining their grip on power. The same billionaires who exploit workers, suppress wages, and hoard wealth are the ones funding right-wing Christian organizations, pouring money into think tanks, lobbying groups, and media networks that push their theocratic agenda. Because they understand something fundamental: a divided, fearful, religiously indoctrinated population is much easier to control than an educated, empowered, secular one.

And so, they create moral panics. They stir up outrage over gender, race, sexuality, anything to distract from the fact that they are robbing the country blind. They convince struggling working-class Christians that their enemy is not the billionaire stripping their community of resources, but the queer couple down the street. They tell women that feminism has made them miserable while ensuring that their economic policies
90

keep women trapped in cycles of poverty. They sell the illusion of religious persecution, convincing white evangelicals, who control every lever of power in this country, that they are the real victims.

This is the Christian nationalist shield. It is not faith, not morality, not righteousness. It is a con. A tool of oppression. A justification for cruelty. And until people see it for what it really is, until they reject the illusion and recognize that this is not about religion but about power, the oppression will continue. Christian nationalism does not need to be believed to be effective, it only needs to be obeyed. But obedience is a choice. And the moment people refuse, the shield cracks, the illusion falls apart, and the entire system built on lies and fear begins to collapse.

The war being waged under the banner of Christian nationalism is not just about policy or ideology, it is about the systematic destruction of autonomy and self-determination. It is about transforming the government into an extension of an extremist religious agenda that seeks to remake society in its own rigid, hierarchical, patriarchal image. It is about taking the language of faith and twisting it into a blunt-force weapon, designed not to uplift or inspire but to subjugate and terrorize. And at the heart of this authoritarian crusade is the forced birth movement, a project so cruel, so rooted in misogyny and domination, that it stands as one of the most grotesque manifestations of modern theocratic rule.

Forced birth laws are not about saving lives. If they were, their architects would be fighting just as hard for universal healthcare, childcare, paid family leave, and social safety nets that ensure children can actually survive once they are born. But these people have no interest in life beyond its use as a tool of coercion. What they want is a society in which pregnancy is not a choice but an obligation, where women and girls are stripped of their bodily autonomy and placed under state control. They want to resurrect the centuries-old notion that women exist to serve as vessels, their bodies mere instruments for fulfilling a patriarchal vision of reproduction and social order. They want to eliminate any possibility that women can live independently of male authority.

The irony is that these laws do not just target women in the abstract, they victimize children. When a 10-year-old rape victim was forced to flee Ohio to obtain an abortion, the so-called "pro-life" movement had no sympathy. They did not express horror at what had happened to her. Instead, they attacked the doctor who helped her, questioned whether her story was even real, and then doubled down on their policies. Because to them, this was not a tragedy, it was a success. Their vision of society demands that victims suffer in silence, that their trauma be ignored, that their bodies remain under the control of the state and the church. These laws were written with full knowledge that they would force children to carry pregnancies to term. And their authors did not care.

Christian nationalists do not care about the suffering of the people they claim to protect. They do not care about the girls and women who will be forced to endure the horrors of pregnancy after rape. They do not care about the medical complications, the lifelong trauma, the deaths that will result from their policies. Because to them, suffering is not a bug in the system, it is the system. It is the price women must pay for existing. They preach that women must be submissive, that they must bear their burdens with grace, that they must see their own subjugation as a divine command. And if they resist? If they seek to control their own bodies, their own destinies? Then they must be punished.

The forced birth agenda is not separate from the larger goals of Christian nationalism, it is central to them. These laws are not isolated policies but part of a broader effort to enshrine religious extremism into the legal system. By criminalizing abortion, they lay the groundwork for criminalizing contraception. By rolling back reproductive rights, they open

92

the door to rolling back women's rights in general. They have already begun targeting no-fault divorce, LGBTQ rights, and laws protecting women from domestic abuse. Because their goal is not just to ban abortion. Their goal is to dismantle the entire framework of gender equality that has been built over the last century.

This is why they call for the repeal of the Equal Rights Amendment. This is why they attack Title IX protections for women and girls. This is why they push policies that allow employers to discriminate based on gender and sexuality under the guise of "religious freedom." This is why they elevate men who openly espouse "traditional gender roles" that amount to little more than a return to legal servitude for women. They are not just trying to control reproduction, they are trying to control every aspect of women's lives.

And the hypocrisy is staggering. The same people who claim to be defenders of family values are the ones pushing for policies that make it harder for families to survive. They fight against paid maternity leave. They cut funding for food assistance and housing support. They block universal childcare. They do everything in their power to ensure that the very women they force into motherhood are left without any resources to care for the children they are made to have. This is not a movement that values life, it is a movement that values punishment. It is about making sure that women who refuse to comply with their fundamentalist vision of gender roles suffer for it.

Christian nationalists know that in order to make their policies stick, they need a moral justification. That is why they have worked so hard to frame their agenda as a battle between good and evil, as a divine war in which they are the righteous warriors defending civilization from collapse. They claim that allowing women to control their own bodies is a rebellion against God's plan. They insist that access to abortion is not just a policy debate but a spiritual battle. They speak in apocalyptic terms, warning that unless their theocratic laws are enforced, society itself will crumble.

But here's the truth: it is not abortion that destroys societies, it is forced birth. It is not gender equality that leads to instability, it is the subjugation of half the population. It is not secular governance that threatens democracy, it is Christian nationalism itself, which seeks to dismantle democracy and replace it with authoritarian religious rule.

The historical parallels are impossible to ignore. Every theocratic regime in history has used religious justification to enforce systems of control. The Puritans burned women as witches for stepping outside of prescribed gender roles. The Catholic Church used the Inquisition to silence dissenters and maintain religious authority. The Taliban enforces strict Sharia law to keep women out of public life. The modern Christian nationalist movement is no different. They do not call their opponents heretics anymore, they call them "woke." They do not burn people at the stake, they criminalize their existence, strip them of their rights, and turn them into political scapegoats. But the result is the same: control, oppression, the destruction of freedom under the guise of divine will.

And just as in past theocracies, those at the top are exempt from the rules they impose. The very men pushing for forced birth laws have mistresses, affairs, secret abortions, hidden scandals that reveal their total lack of sincerity. They preach abstinence while indulging in excess. They claim to be defenders of purity while protecting abusers and rapists. They use religion as a shield, not because they believe in it, but because they know it gives them power. They are not men of faith. They are men of greed, cruelty, and domination, hiding behind the Bible to justify their reign.

Christian nationalism thrives on a culture of silence. It needs people to be afraid to speak out, to question, to resist. It relies on shame, on guilt, on the idea that challenging religious authority is the same as challenging God. But here's the truth: Christian nationalism is not Christianity. It is a political movement, a corporate-funded, billionaire-backed effort to turn religion into a weapon of oppression. It is not about faith, it is about control. And the only way to defeat it is to refuse to let that control continue.

This fight is not just about abortion. It is not just about reproductive rights. It is about whether or not we allow religious extremists to dictate the laws that govern us all. It is about whether or not we let a fanatical minority remake the country in its own cruel image. It is about whether or not we accept a world where women and girls are stripped of their autonomy and forced into a future dictated by men who see them as nothing more than property.

The Christian nationalist shield is cracking. The lies are unraveling. And the more people see these laws for what they really are, not about life, not about morality, but about control, the harder it will be for them to enforce their theocratic vision. The question is not whether they will stop. They will not. The question is whether we will stop them. And that is a question that must be answered now.

Death of Democracy/ Rise of Pervertocracy

Democracy wasn't taken down in some dramatic coup, with tanks in the streets and flags waving in the ashes of the old order. No, that would've been too obvious. Too messy. Instead, it was disassembled piece by piece, law by law, election by election, until one day we woke up and realized it was gone. Not dead in a way that could be mourned and buried, but gutted, hollowed out, its rotting corpse paraded around to keep up the illusion that the people still had a voice. The truth is, democracy didn't collapse, it was stolen, sold off to the highest bidders, and now it's locked behind private security gates where the rich and powerful get to play king while the rest of us get to fight over the scraps. And who orchestrated this slow-motion robbery? The perverts. The ones who salivate at control, who see governance not as a duty but as an opportunity to mold the world into their personal playground.

They've spent decades perfecting the con, wrapping their greed in patriotism, their authoritarianism in religious sanctimony, their perversion of morality in legal jargon so convoluted the public barely realizes they're being screwed. They don't kick down the front door and declare democracy over. No, they chip away at it, one vote suppressed here, one public institution gutted there, until all that's left is a glorified auction house where policies go to the highest bidder and politicians are nothing more than corporate sales reps in cheap suits. And the beauty of their scheme? They've managed to convince the public that this is what democracy *looks like*. That the people who make all the decisions being wealthy, white, male, and utterly detached from reality is somehow just the natural order of things. That being given the illusion of choice between two pre-approved, corporate-funded candidates every four years is enough to call this a functioning system.

But it's not just about money and power. That's too simple. If it were just a matter of greed, they'd be satisfied with controlling the economy. No, this is something deeper, darker. It's about domination. It's about making sure that people don't just lose power, they forget they ever had it. They break systems, declare them failures, and then swoop in with privatized "solutions" that do nothing but consolidate control in fewer and fewer hands. Education? They gutted public schools, then funneled billions into charter networks run by their friends. Healthcare? They let hospitals close, doctors burn out, people die waiting for basic care, then told us the only fix was to let the insurance companies, already bloated beyond reason, have even more power. Elections? They gerrymandered districts into unrecognizable shapes, purged voter rolls, made it harder to vote in every way possible, then called it "security." Each failure they manufacture becomes another excuse to seize more control, funnel more money to their own, and strip more power from the people.

And the gaslighting. Oh, the gaslighting is a work of art. Because for all the destruction they unleash, they never take responsibility. Instead, they turn to the people they've just screwed over and say, *See? Government doesn't work.* They break it, they wreck it, they burn it down, and then they point at the smoldering ruins and demand that everything be handed over to the private sector, their private sector. This is how you end up with billionaires running schools, hedge funds owning hospitals, and corporations writing the laws that regulate themselves. And every time it fails, because it always fails, the answer is never to take power back from them. No, the answer is always to hand over even more, to deregulate further, to privatize deeper, to concentrate wealth and control until there's nothing left to take.
98

Look at how they handle crisis. Every disaster, whether it's economic, environmental, or political, becomes an excuse to consolidate power. When the economy collapses, they bail out banks while regular people lose their homes. When a pandemic strikes, they funnel public money into corporate pockets, leaving small businesses and workers to fend for themselves. When climate disasters devastate communities, they sell off resources to the highest bidder and let the displaced figure it out on their own. It's disaster capitalism at its finest, the ability to profit from failure, to turn human suffering into an investment opportunity. They don't just thrive in chaos; they create it. And they've managed to convince millions that the only way out of this mess is to trust the very people who orchestrated it.

And then there's the moral angle. The great perversion of values, where these same people claim to be the defenders of faith, of tradition, of family. They wrap themselves in religious rhetoric, spewing sanctimonious drivel about decency and righteousness, while their policies strip rights away from women, deny children food and education, and create a society where the only people who truly thrive are those who already have everything. They scream about government tyranny while quietly making sure that corporations have more power over our daily lives than any elected official ever could. They wail about religious freedom while ensuring that only *their* version of religion gets to dictate law and policy. They talk about preserving the American way of life while gutting every protection that once made life even *remotely* fair for working people.

The perverts running this show don't just want money. They want obedience. They want a population too exhausted, too beaten down, too demoralized to fight back. They want a country where people don't dream of something better because they can't even remember what "better" looks like. They want the public so distracted by survival, by manufactured culture wars, by bread and circus politics, that no one notices the slow, methodical takeover of everything that once made democracy real. And they've been wildly successful. They've normalized the absurd. They've convinced people that endless war, mass homelessness, collapsing healthcare, poisoned water, and debt servitude are all just part of living in a "free" country. They've made it seem radical to suggest that basic human dignity shouldn't have a price tag.

And through it all, they maintain their perverted smiles, insisting that this is what freedom looks like. That this is what democracy is supposed to be. That voting every few years for candidates who have already been bought and sold is the height of civic engagement. That if you're struggling, if you're drowning under medical debt, if you're working three jobs to survive, if you're watching your kids' futures shrink before your eyes, it's not *their* fault. It's yours. Work harder. Stop complaining. Be grateful for what you have, even as they take the last of it from you.

They have turned democracy into a Pervertocracy, a system where the most corrupt, the most depraved, the most morally bankrupt rise to the top and dictate the rules for everyone else. A system where justice is a commodity, where freedom is a corporate slogan, where the right to live a decent life is treated as a privilege for the few rather than a right for all. They have replaced public good with private gain, governance with greed, representation with repression. And the scariest part? They've done it so slowly, so expertly, so insidiously, that most people don't even realize what's been lost.

But it's not gone. Not yet. Because the one thing they can never fully erase is the possibility of opposition. And if there's one thing they fear, it's that people might finally see through the illusion, might finally recognize the scam for what it is, might finally decide they've had enough. Because when that happens, when people wake up, when they start fighting back, the perverts at the top won't know what hit them. And that's why they fight so hard to keep the lie alive. To keep the system

100

rigged. To keep us divided, distracted, and too exhausted to resist. Because they know the truth, even if they'll never say it out loud: their power only lasts as long as we let them have it.

The pervertocracy doesn't just dismantle democracy; it replaces it with something far worse, a grotesque system where power is concentrated in the hands of the most corrupt, the most shameless, the most willing to lie, steal, and manipulate their way to the top. And it's not just about winning elections or passing laws. No, these perverts want to rewrite the very concept of governance itself, making it indistinguishable from corporate dominance, where everything is transactional, and the people, the actual citizens, are nothing more than a captive market.

They don't govern in any real sense. That would require a sense of duty, of responsibility, of accountability. Instead, they rule, and they do it in the most obscene way possible, by making sure the institutions meant to serve the public are so broken, so inefficient, so humiliating to interact with that people start to believe the only solution is to hand everything over to private interests. This is why you wait on hold for three hours to talk to the IRS but can open a credit card account in five minutes. It's why public schools crumble while charter school executives collect multi-million-dollar bonuses. It's why the post office gets gutted while Amazon expands into every inch of daily life. The message is always the same: *government doesn't work, so let the corporations take over.* But here's the catch, government doesn't work *because they broke it on purpose.* They defund, deregulate, obstruct, and sabotage, and then they stand back and smirk while people suffer, pointing at the mess and saying, *See? We told you so.*

And once the system is weak enough, they move in. Education becomes a profit center, with private schools and charter networks sucking up public money while producing worse outcomes. Healthcare becomes a financial racket, where insurance companies decide who lives and who dies based on algorithms designed to maximize shareholder returns. The prison system turns into a human meat grinder, a source of cheap labor for private corporations that pay pennies per hour while charging the government thousands per inmate. Even the military, once an unquestioned arm of the state, is now riddled with privatized mercenary armies, security firms, and weapons contractors whose primary interest isn't national defense, it's keeping the war machine running, because peace is bad for business.

But privatization is only half the story. The real power of the pervertocracy is in its ability to make democracy feel meaningless. If people believe their vote doesn't count, their voice doesn't matter, and their efforts to change things are futile, they'll stop participating altogether. And that's the goal. Voter suppression isn't just about keeping certain people from the polls; it's about making the entire process so disillusioning, so exhausting, that people disengage entirely. They want apathy. They need cynicism. Because the fewer people who believe in democracy, the easier it is to control.

Take gerrymandering. These perverts have redrawn district maps into twisted, nonsensical shapes, ensuring that politicians choose their voters rather than the other way around. They've created a system where a party can lose the popular vote by millions and still hold onto power. And then they have the audacity to turn around and tell people that if they don't like the way things are, they should just "vote harder." As if the game isn't already rigged. As if the courts, stacked with handpicked ideological extremists, aren't ready to strike down any policy that threatens their control. As if the Electoral College, that relic of slavery and aristocratic rule, isn't in place specifically to prevent actual democracy from taking hold.

And it's not just elections. They've redefined protest itself as an act of terrorism. Peaceful demonstrators are met with militarized police forces, tear gas, and mass arrests, while the actual insurrectionists, the ones who stormed the Capitol in
102

broad daylight, are treated as misguided patriots. The message is clear: only some forms of dissent are acceptable, and only certain people are allowed to challenge authority. If you're protesting for higher wages, environmental protections, or racial justice, you're a threat. If you're breaking into government buildings to overturn an election in favor of corporate fascism, you're a hero. This isn't hypocrisy; it's the blueprint for authoritarian rule.

But the greatest trick of all is how they manipulate language itself. They don't come out and say they're dismantling democracy. They say they're protecting *election integrity*. They don't admit they're handing public goods over to their corporate friends. They call it *free market solutions*. They don't announce that they're stripping women, workers, and marginalized communities of their rights. They say they're fighting *wokeness*, protecting *traditional values*, or ensuring *religious liberty*. Everything is a smokescreen, designed to keep the public confused, distracted, and too exhausted to resist.

And let's talk about exhaustion. Because that's another one of their weapons, grinding people down until they don't have the energy to fight back. Keeping wages low, healthcare expensive, and education unaffordable isn't just about profit. It's about control. If you're working three jobs just to survive, you don't have time to organize. If you're buried in medical debt, you don't have the bandwidth to focus on systemic corruption. If you're constantly afraid of losing your home, your job, or your future, you're not going to risk sticking your neck out. And they know this. They *depend* on it. A desperate, struggling population is an obedient one. A population that can't afford to take a day off work to protest is a population that won't revolt.

The final nail in the coffin of democracy is the illusion of debate. The constant back-and-forth, the staged arguments on cable news, the endless cycle of outrage, it's all part of the game. Because as long as people are arguing over surface-level nonsense, they're not paying attention to the bigger picture.

The politicians on both sides get on TV, wag their fingers at each other, and act like they're engaged in some grand ideological battle, when in reality, they're both just different brands of the same product. The pervertocracy isn't about left versus right. It's about top versus bottom. And as long as the people at the bottom keep fighting each other, the ones at the top keep winning.

They've mastered the art of making people beg for their own oppression. They convince voters that universal healthcare is an impossible dream while quietly handing billions in subsidies to the insurance industry. They tell us that student loan forgiveness is too expensive while bailing out banks and corporations without a second thought. They make people fear "big government" while creating a system where the only real choices are between corporate overlords, one set with a blue logo, the other with a red.

And that's how democracy dies. Not with a bang, not with a dictator seizing power in a dramatic coup, but with a slow, deliberate erosion of every system designed to hold the powerful accountable. It dies when people stop believing their voices matter. It dies when they lose faith in institutions that were never meant to serve them in the first place. It dies when the public is too tired, too beaten down, and too distracted to fight back.

But here's the thing: it's not dead yet. And that's what they fear the most. Because the only thing that can stop the pervertocracy is a population that refuses to accept it. A population that sees through the lies, that recognizes the con, that understands democracy isn't something given, it's something taken, built, fought for. They want us to believe we're powerless, because the moment we realize we're not, their grip starts to slip.

That's why they push so hard to keep us divided, to keep us exhausted, to keep us arguing over crumbs while they feast at the table. Because they know that if we ever turn our attention to them, really, truly focus on what they're doing, their game is over. And for all their power, all their money, all their control, there's one thing they still can't fully destroy: the possibility of opposition. The chance that, one day, enough people will say *enough*. And that's why they fight so hard. Because they know, deep down, that the people still have the power to take it all back.

They've spent decades convincing us that democracy is still alive while they hollowed it out, leaving behind a cheap stage set where elections are bought, laws are written by corporate lobbyists, and the courts are stocked with ideological extremists whose only real job is to rubber-stamp the destruction of public power. The pervertocracy doesn't just want control, they want obedience. They want the people to be so demoralized, so exhausted, so hopeless that they accept this nightmare as normal. But here's the thing about control: it's never absolute. No matter how many institutions they break, no matter how many rights they strip away, no matter how many distractions they throw at the public, the one thing they can never fully erase is the possibility of resistance.

And that terrifies them.

The perverts in charge, the billionaires, the politicians, the religious extremists, the corporate overlords, they know that their entire system is built on deception. They know that if people ever stop believing in their manufactured narratives, if they stop accepting the way things are and start demanding something better, the whole thing comes crashing down. That's why they push propaganda so relentlessly, why they flood the airwaves with fearmongering, why they spend billions on think tanks and media outlets designed to keep people disoriented and compliant. They don't want an informed public. They don't want engaged citizens. They want a consumer class, a desperate workforce, an exhausted population too busy trying to survive to ever think about fighting back.

So they build their control mechanisms carefully, ensuring that every system that could be used against them is either co-opted or destroyed. The media, once meant to be the watchdog of democracy, has been turned into a corporate circus where real issues are buried under manufactured culture wars and endless sensationalism. Education, which should be a tool for empowerment, has been transformed into an assembly line that churns out obedient workers saddled with mountains of debt. The legal system, meant to provide justice, has been twisted into a weapon for the rich and a cage for the poor, where billionaires skate free after laundering money and committing fraud while a single mother can lose her children because she can't afford a traffic ticket.

And worst of all, they make sure that any attempt to change this system is met with the same response: suppression, vilification, and, if necessary, violence. Protesters are beaten, arrested, and labeled as terrorists. Whistleblowers exposing corporate and government corruption are exiled or imprisoned. Workers organizing for better wages are threatened, fired, or worse. They cannot allow any real challenge to their rule, so they treat every act of defiance, no matter how small, as an existential threat.

And they're not entirely wrong.

Because the thing they fear the most isn't a single protest, a single election, or a single movement. It's the realization, spreading like cracks in their carefully controlled system, that people aren't as powerless as they've been led to believe. That democracy, even in its broken state, still contains the embers of something real. That the pervertocracy, for all its money and all its control, still relies on one thing: public submission. And once the public refuses to submit, their power starts to crumble.

This is why they lean so hard into division. They stoke racial animosity, gender wars, and ideological battles not because they actually care about these things but because they know that if people ever unite against them, they lose. They encourage people to blame immigrants, to fear their neighbors, to see every struggle in zero-sum terms, because as long as the people are fighting each other, they're not fighting the system. This is the oldest trick in the book, and yet it works again and again, because when people are desperate, they reach for easy answers. And the pervertocracy is always ready to provide them.

But even this strategy has its limits. Because there comes a point where people, no matter how conditioned, no matter how exhausted, start to see through the illusion. There comes a moment where the suffering becomes too obvious, the contradictions too blatant, the lies too transparent. And when that happens, change becomes inevitable.

We've seen it before. Every major movement for justice, from labor rights to civil rights to suffrage, was met with the same weapons of suppression, the same tactics of division, the same declarations that change was impossible. And yet, change came. Not because those in power allowed it, but because the people demanded it. And if history has taught us anything, it's that no system, no matter how powerful, no matter how entrenched, can withstand the full weight of collective defiance.

The pervertocracy wants people to believe that resistance is futile. That the rich will always rule, that the powerful will always exploit, that democracy, real democracy, was a fluke, an accident of history that has now been corrected. They want people to believe that the only thing they can do is adjust, adapt, and accept their fate.

But that's the lie.

The truth is that democracy is not something that can be handed down from above, it has to be built from below. It is not a fixed institution; it is an ongoing struggle. And that struggle is never over. The perverts in power will never stop

trying to consolidate control, but the people will never stop
resisting. It's the eternal battle between oppression and
freedom, between hoarded power and collective power,
between the few who rule and the many who refuse to be ruled.

And make no mistake: the pervertocracy can be dismantled.
Their entire system is built on smoke and mirrors, on keeping
people too distracted, too beaten down, too afraid to fight back.
The moment people stop playing by their rules, the moment
they realize they don't have to accept this as normal, the whole
house of cards starts to shake.

So the question isn't *if* democracy can be restored. The
question is whether enough people are willing to fight for it. To
see through the gaslighting, to reject the manufactured
divisions, to recognize that the real battle isn't left versus right
but the people versus the powerful. To stop waiting for saviors
and start organizing. To stop asking for permission and start
demanding justice.

The perverts running this system aren't invincible. They aren't
gods. They aren't even particularly smart. They're just ruthless,
greedy, and lucky enough to have convinced an entire nation
that their rule is inevitable.
It's not.

Democracy didn't die. It was stolen. And it can be taken back.
But only if we're willing to stop letting them tell us that we're
powerless.

~10
Exposing the Perverts and the Virus

The perverts and the greed virus thrive in darkness. They count on secrecy, manipulation, and a carefully controlled narrative to maintain their grip on power. Their survival depends on distraction, on making sure people are too overwhelmed, too divided, too exhausted to pay attention to what's really happening. Because once the public sees them for what they are, once their grotesque behaviors, their lies, their hoarding of wealth and power are dragged into the open, their entire foundation starts to crack. Exposure is their greatest fear. It's why they control the media, why they bury real stories under an avalanche of manufactured outrage, why they brand every critic as dangerous, radical, or unhinged. But the truth is the most dangerous weapon against them, and it's time to wield it.

There's no one way to expose them. The greed virus has mutated across industries, governments, and religious institutions, each infected host using different tactics to disguise their corruption. The billionaires who rob the public while playing philanthropist. The politicians who strip away rights while proclaiming themselves defenders of freedom. The media moguls who flood the airwaves with propaganda while quietly selling the public's attention to the highest bidder. The theocrats who preach morality while covering up their own depravity. Each requires a different strategy, but all of them share the same weakness: the moment people see through the illusion, the spell is broken.

And that's where storytelling comes in. The perverts control
the official narrative. They rewrite history, frame the present,
and predict a future where their dominance is inevitable. They
flood every available space with distractions, manufactured
culture wars, trivial scandals, meaningless debates, so that no
one notices the bigger con. Their version of events always casts
them as the heroes, the self-made titans of industry, the noble
stewards of democracy, the defenders of faith and tradition.
Their greed isn't greed, it's *job creation*. Their corruption isn't
corruption, it's *the free market at work*. Their cruelty isn't cruelty,
it's *necessary discipline*.

But the truth is ugly, and when people see it laid bare, the effect
is undeniable. It's not enough to list statistics or facts, the
brainwashed masses won't absorb them. The truth needs to hit
in the gut, in the emotions. That's why storytelling, using
humor, satire, and pointed exposure, is one of the most
powerful tools of resistance.

Consider how they react when their hypocrisy is made obvious.
When a televangelist preaches against sin while getting caught
with a mistress. When a pro-life politician forces his mistress to
get an abortion. When a CEO who lobbied against healthcare
expansion suddenly begs for public assistance when he gets
sick. These moments expose the fraud, the perversion of
morality, the sheer absurdity of their entire belief system. And
that's why they try so hard to bury those stories, to spin the
narrative, to make sure that people quickly move on to the next
distraction before the realization fully sets in.

The key to exposing them is to hold on to these stories, to
amplify them, to make sure people don't forget. It's about
connecting the dots, making the patterns undeniable. One
corrupt politician can be dismissed as a bad apple. But when it
happens again, and again, and again, people start to see that
it's not just a fluke, it's the system itself.

This is why satire is so effective. Laughter, when wielded correctly, is a weapon. It cuts through the illusion, reveals the grotesque, makes it impossible to look away. Satire exposes not just the hypocrisy, but the sheer ridiculousness of it all. The billionaires building doomsday bunkers while telling the rest of us to "work harder." The politicians screaming about "family values" while covering up abuse scandals. The hedge fund managers looting pensions while telling the poor they should have planned better. When framed correctly, their entire ideology collapses under its own weight.

And that's why they hate being laughed at. These people, so drunk on power, so convinced of their own importance, cannot stand mockery. They expect to be feared, respected, worshipped even. They want the public to see them as larger than life, as figures of authority, as gods walking among men. But the moment they are ridiculed, their power shrinks. The emperor has no clothes, and once people see it, they can never unsee it.

But satire alone isn't enough. The truth has to be hammered into the public consciousness over and over again, because the perverts and their propaganda machines will do everything they can to bury it. Every time their corruption is exposed, they flood the news cycle with distractions. A celebrity scandal. A manufactured outrage. A new enemy to fear. They will do *anything* to shift the narrative, to make people forget, to keep the attention elsewhere. And the only way to fight that is with relentless exposure.

Take corporate greed, for example. The way these companies jack up prices under the excuse of inflation while making record profits. The way they lay off workers while rewarding their executives with massive bonuses. The way they buy up competitors, monopolize industries, then gaslight the public into believing there's still competition. This is theft on a massive scale, but the perverts running these companies have perfected the art of making it seem normal, even necessary.

They flood the media with talking points, blaming workers, blaming consumers, blaming *anyone* but themselves. And it works, unless people make sure it doesn't.

This is why activism must go hand in hand with exposure. Once the truth is out, there has to be action. Organized boycotts, strikes, protests, campaigns to publicly shame the worst offenders. These methods have been used before, successfully. But they only work when people stay focused, when they don't let themselves be distracted, when they refuse to let the perverts regain control of the narrative.

And that's the hardest part. Because the perverts are experts at making people feel powerless. They've spent years perfecting the art of demoralization, convincing the public that nothing can be done, that they are too strong, too rich, too entrenched to be challenged. This is their greatest trick. The lie they repeat endlessly. But it's just that, a lie.

History proves it. Every empire falls. Every tyrant meets their end. Every system that hoards too much power, that exploits too many people, eventually collapses under the weight of its own greed. It's not a question of *if*, it's a question of *when*. And the perverts know this. That's why they fight so hard to keep the public distracted, divided, exhausted. They know that the moment people actually unite, actually focus, actually refuse to accept this system any longer, it's over for them.

The goal of exposure is to accelerate that realization. To rip the mask off the perverts before they have a chance to slip another one on. To ensure that their lies, their crimes, their grotesque behaviors remain burned into public consciousness. To make it impossible for them to hide.

And that starts with recognizing that the battle isn't just in elections or policy. It's in the stories we tell, the narratives we reinforce, the way we frame reality itself. The perverts count on controlling perception, because perception shapes reality. But if

114

enough people refuse to buy into their manufactured world, if enough people call them out, laugh at them, expose them, demand consequences, then reality starts to shift.

The perverts can only rule for as long as people believe they have the right to. Exposure is about shattering that belief, making it clear that they are not invincible, that their power is not ordained, that their grotesque empire is built on nothing but deceit and theft.

And once people see the truth, really see it, there's no going back. The perverts can run, they can spin, they can try to hide behind their money and their media, but it won't matter. Because when the virus is exposed, it can finally be eradicated. And that's what they fear most of all.

The perverts and the greed virus don't just rely on secrecy to maintain power, they depend on manipulation, distraction, and a carefully orchestrated performance designed to keep the public confused and demoralized. It's not enough for them to steal wealth, hoard resources, and consolidate control; they also have to make sure no one fights back in a way that actually threatens their rule. That's why exposure alone isn't enough. It has to be *relentless*. It has to be woven into culture, into satire, into resistance movements that refuse to let their crimes and hypocrisy fade into the background noise of the next news cycle. They count on outrage fatigue. They know that people can only stay furious for so long before exhaustion sets in, before the constant barrage of corruption and cruelty starts to feel normal. That's their trick, to keep pushing the line, to keep escalating, until people lose the will to fight. But the moment people recognize the pattern, the moment they see the long con for what it is, the spell starts to break.

One of the biggest tools of exposure is satire. Because nothing destroys power faster than ridicule. The perverts crave respect, reverence, fear. They want to be seen as the all-knowing masters of the universe, as the job creators, the moral authorities, the economic geniuses. But in reality, they are just thieves in expensive suits, sociopaths in positions of unchecked authority, charlatans who have tricked the world into believing that their obscene wealth and power are deserved. And when you strip away their carefully crafted image and expose them for the ridiculous, bloated, self-obsessed perverts they are, their legitimacy crumbles. That's why they lash out at comedians. That's why they hate mockery. That's why they fear any narrative that makes them look weak, foolish, or out of touch. They can handle anger. They *feed* off division. But what they cannot stand is being made to look like fools.

Take the billionaires who build bunkers in New Zealand to escape the consequences of their own greed. They know climate collapse is coming. They know economic instability is inevitable. And instead of using their power and wealth to prevent it, they hoard resources and prepare to flee. This isn't leadership. This isn't genius. It's cowardice. It's pathetic. And when that reality is framed in the right way, when their paranoia and self-preservation instincts are exposed for what they are, it becomes impossible for them to maintain their illusion of superiority. They go from untouchable titans to scared little men, stockpiling canned goods and hiring private security teams to protect them from the collapse *they caused.* They become the joke. And once they're the joke, their power starts to weaken.

And it's not just billionaires. The politicians who enforce this system of greed and corruption, who gut public institutions while stuffing their own pockets, need to be dragged into the light, too. They rely on coded language, on vague justifications, on a political performance that makes them appear like serious statesmen rather than corporate lackeys. They stand on stages and talk about "cutting red tape" when what they really mean is stripping workers of their protections, making it easier for corporations to pollute, ensuring that the rich never have to answer for their crimes. They call it "fiscal responsibility" when what they mean is funneling money from public programs into

116

the pockets of their billionaire donors. They say they're fighting for "family values" while they protect rapists, defend child marriage, and strip away reproductive rights. Their entire language is a lie. And exposing them means refusing to play along. It means calling them what they are, liars, thieves, and perverts who wield power not to serve the public, but to control and exploit.

But exposure is about more than just pointing out hypocrisy. Because the truth is, these people don't *care* if they're called hypocrites. They don't care if they're caught lying. They don't care if their scandals are uncovered, if their cruelty is exposed. If they did, they wouldn't still be in power. No, the real goal of exposure isn't just to reveal corruption, it's to make sure the public *doesn't forget*. That's why movements have to be relentless. That's why every scandal, every grotesque abuse of power, every moment of corruption needs to be hammered into public consciousness, repeated again and again until it becomes impossible to ignore.

Take corporate greedflation, for example. When the pandemic hit, people were scared, struggling, dying. And what did corporations do? They jacked up prices on everything. Not because of supply chain issues, not because they had to, but because they *could*. They took advantage of crisis, of fear, of suffering, and they used it as an opportunity to make record profits. And when they got called out, what did they do? They blamed inflation. They blamed workers. They blamed the government. Anything to avoid admitting the truth: that they were *looting* the public in broad daylight. And here's the worst part, people *almost* forgot. Because new distractions emerged. New crises, new headlines, new culture wars designed to keep the conversation moving forward, away from the fact that these corporations *stole* from the people while they were at their most vulnerable.

But that's where resistance comes in. Because the moment people refuse to let go, the moment they keep hammering the point, keep making it clear that this wasn't an accident or a necessary evil but *theft*, the perverts start to panic. That's when they start calling for unity, for civility. That's when they start playing the victim, acting like they're being unfairly targeted. That's when they start changing the narrative, pretending they care about the very people they just finished robbing.

And that's the sign of progress. Because if they're scrambling to shift the conversation, it means they're losing control of it.

The same applies to politics. Every time they break a system, they blame the people it was meant to serve. They gut public education, then point to underfunded schools as proof that public education doesn't work. They slash social services, then claim welfare makes people lazy. They create crime by fostering poverty, then use that crime to justify mass incarceration. Every single failure they manufacture becomes an argument for more privatization, more deregulation, more control in their hands. And every time they do it, they count on the public forgetting that *they* are the ones who caused the problem in the first place.

That's why exposure isn't just about pointing out their crimes, it's about making sure people *remember*. It's about keeping a record of their lies, their theft, their destruction, so that the next time they try to pull the same trick, they can't get away with it.

And most importantly, it's about making it *personal.* Because the perverts and the greed virus don't just destroy democracy in the abstract. They don't just harm some distant, faceless public. They hurt *real people.* The mother who lost her child because she was denied an abortion. The worker who died on the job because safety regulations were "too expensive." The family who lost their home because a hedge fund decided to hike rent beyond what they could afford. These aren't numbers. These aren't statistics. These are lives, and when people see that, when they *feel* it, the lies of the perverts start to lose their power.

And that's what exposure is really about. Not just information. Not just calling out corruption. But making sure that people *see* the truth, *feel* the truth, and refuse to look away. Because the moment enough people do that, the pervertocracy begins to crumble. And no amount of wealth, power, or propaganda can stop it.

The perverts who rule this system, these political, corporate, and religious frauds, are masters of evasion. They do not acknowledge consequences, they do not engage with criticism in good faith, and they certainly do not take responsibility for the destruction they cause. They do not apologize, because they do not believe they should have to. Instead, when exposed, they double down. They shift blame. They launch new distractions. They cry victim while continuing to prey on the people they've already stolen from. They build their power on the assumption that no one will remember their last lie, their last scandal, their last act of brutality. That's why the final phase of exposure isn't just about documenting their crimes, it's about making sure they *never escape them.*

There's a reason why they control the media. There's a reason why every billionaire wants to own a news network, a tech platform, a publishing empire. It's not enough for them to commit crimes in broad daylight, they also need the ability to rewrite the record, to erase the evidence, to shift the public's focus onto something else before the truth has time to sink in. They understand something fundamental about human nature: memory is fragile. If people aren't constantly reminded of how they've been robbed, cheated, and manipulated, they'll move on. They'll adjust. They'll accept the latest outrage as just another part of life, another unavoidable aspect of the modern world. And once that happens, the perverts win.

This is why control of information is their first and final battleground. The greed virus spreads most efficiently through silence. It thrives when workers don't know how they're being exploited, when renters don't understand why their housing is unaffordable, when voters don't realize how thoroughly their political system has been rigged. That's why whistleblowers are treated as criminals, why journalists who expose corruption end up in exile or in prison, why movements that challenge corporate power are relentlessly smeared as dangerous, radical, or "bad for the economy." It's not just about protecting their wealth, it's about ensuring that people *never see the full picture.*

And that means exposing them isn't just about revealing individual crimes, it's about countering their entire system of propaganda, dismantling the narratives they've carefully built to justify their rule. It's about reminding people that what is happening to them is not normal, not inevitable, not something they just have to accept. That every manufactured crisis, every fabricated economic downturn, every rollback of rights is not some act of fate, it is a deliberate choice made by those who hold power.

Think about how they frame economic policy. Whenever wages stagnate, whenever unemployment spikes, whenever healthcare costs spiral out of control, the perverts and their mouthpieces flood the media with the same tired excuses. *It's just market forces. It's inflation. It's the result of too much government spending.* They always have an answer, a justification, a way to make the public believe that the crushing weight of economic hardship is a force of nature rather than a direct result of policy choices made by the ruling class. And because they repeat these lies so often, because they spread them across every available platform, people start to believe them. Even the people suffering the most start to internalize the idea that their poverty, their debt, their inability to afford basic necessities is *their fault.*

This is why exposing the greed virus requires breaking the cycle of manufactured consent. It requires disrupting the constant flood of misinformation that keeps people in a state of confusion, frustration, and resignation. And it starts with cutting through the noise, hammering home, over and over

120

again, that every financial crisis is a scam, that every billionaire's wealth is stolen, that every worker struggling to survive is doing so because the system is designed to keep them that way.

But exposure alone isn't enough. The perverts know that even when they are caught, even when they are exposed, they can still maintain power through one simple trick: impunity. The reason they continue robbing, lying, and cheating isn't because they're brilliant strategists, it's because they know nothing will happen to them. No jail time. No consequences. No accountability. When a billionaire avoids paying taxes, when a corporation poisons the environment, when a politician rigs an election, they don't fear arrest. They don't fear losing power. Because they *own* the institutions that are supposed to hold them accountable.

That's why exposure must be followed by disruption. The system cannot be reformed. It cannot be "fixed" from the inside. It has to be torn apart, root and stem. And the first step to doing that is making sure that the public *refuses to let go of their anger*. That they stop believing in the lie of procedural justice, in the fantasy that if they just vote hard enough, if they just appeal to the better nature of these perverts, things will change. Because they won't.

These people do not have a better nature. They do not govern, they rule. They do not lead, they extract. They do not care about public well-being, national stability, or even the long-term survival of the planet. They only care about how much they can take before the system collapses entirely. And if history has shown us anything, it's that they will not stop until they are forced to stop. So how does that happen?
By ensuring that the public sees them for what they are, not untouchable elites, but parasites. By making it clear that their power exists only because people allow it to exist. By destroying the illusion of inevitability that keeps people from rising up. Every revolution, every mass movement, every historical

moment of real change has started with that realization. The moment people stop believing that their rulers are gods, the moment they stop treating their wealth and power as something deserved rather than stolen, the game is over.

And we are dangerously close to that moment. The perverts know it. That's why they're doubling down on suppression. That's why they're flooding the public sphere with propaganda at an even more frantic pace, why they're trying to rewrite history in real time, why they're expanding police powers, cracking down on dissent, criminalizing protest. They can feel the foundation of their empire shaking beneath them. And that means it's working.

The final phase of exposure is about accelerating that collapse. It's about making sure that every scam, every lie, every theft, every act of violence is remembered, documented, and weaponized against them. It's about stripping them of their ability to hide behind respectability, behind corporate branding, behind the false moral authority they claim for themselves.

Because once they are fully exposed, once people no longer see them as leaders or innovators or visionaries, but as the corrupt, greedy perverts they are, their power begins to erode. They will fight to the bitter end to prevent that from happening. They will throw money at the problem. They will unleash police and military forces. They will expand surveillance, imprison dissenters, rig elections, and rewrite laws to criminalize resistance. But it won't matter.

Because once people see the truth, they will never unsee it. And that is what they fear the most. The perverts and the greed virus can only exist in a world where people accept their rule. Where people believe that the system is unchangeable. Where people stay quiet. But silence is a choice. And it is a choice that, sooner or later, enough people will refuse to make.

Because the perverts, for all their wealth, for all their power, for all their illusions of control, are still just people. And people, no matter how rich, no matter how well-protected, can fall.

They always do.

~11
Fighting the Virus, Healing the World

There is no reforming a system built on exploitation. There is no "fixing" a structure designed to funnel wealth, power, and resources into the hands of a privileged few while the majority suffer. The greed virus has infected every institution, from government to business to religion, twisting them into tools of control, extraction, and destruction. And if we have learned anything from history, it's that when corruption reaches this level, when a system exists solely to sustain the powerful at the expense of everyone else, there is only one path forward: dismantling it entirely.

The perverts who run this system will insist that with the right policies, the right regulations, the right representatives in office, things can be improved. They'll try to convince people that the problems aren't structural but temporary, that with enough patience and compromise, the system can return to some mythical era of balance and fairness. But that is a carefully crafted lie meant to pacify resistance and buy time for the ruling class to reinforce their grip.

The reality is that systemic change requires more than elections, new faces in old offices, or weak, piecemeal reforms. The system itself, the way wealth is hoarded, the way power is structured, the way every aspect of life is controlled by corporate and religious overlords, must be torn out, root and stem, and something radically different must take its place.

At the core of the greed virus is the extreme concentration of wealth. The billionaires, hedge funds, and multinational conglomerates do not simply have more money than everyone else. They own everything, the land, the housing, the factories, the supply chains, the food production, the media, the elections, and the legislative process. They have turned the planet into a resource to be extracted, privatized, and sold back to the very people who built it. As long as this level of control exists, democracy is a fantasy. As long as a handful of individuals and corporations dictate the flow of money, goods, and labor, the idea that people have any real say in how their lives are governed is a cruel joke.

Redistributing wealth is not just an economic necessity; it is a prerequisite for meaningful change. But the perverts will scream "socialism" the moment anyone suggests that billionaires shouldn't exist, that corporations shouldn't be allowed to hoard the necessities of life, that wealth should be used for the collective good rather than private luxury. They will cry about the dangers of "big government" while simultaneously lobbying to ensure that their monopolies remain untouched. They will declare that any attempt to redistribute wealth is an attack on freedom. But whose freedom? Certainly not that of the worker who cannot afford healthcare, or the tenant living under the constant threat of eviction, or the single parent choosing between rent and food. No, the only freedom they care about is their own, the freedom to exploit, to extract, to hoard.

The redistribution of wealth does not mean simply raising taxes or tweaking economic policy to make the system fairer. It means reclaiming stolen resources and returning them to the public. It means breaking up monopolies that have turned entire industries into private kingdoms. It means eliminating the concept of extreme wealth altogether because no single individual should ever have the ability to control the fate of millions simply by virtue of their bank account.

But wealth alone is not enough. The system of corporate and religious control must also be dismantled. The corporate structure as it exists today serves no purpose other than the relentless accumulation of profit, no matter the human or environmental cost. Every major industry, healthcare, agriculture, technology, media, has been swallowed up by corporate monopolies whose only goal is to maximize shareholder returns. These entities do not function within any moral framework; they answer only to profit margins. And they are protected by a legal system designed to shield them from consequences, ensuring that no matter how much harm they cause, they will continue to grow, merge, expand, and dominate.

The only solution is to remove their power entirely. Corporations must be stripped of their influence over government, banned from writing laws, prohibited from funding campaigns, and forced to operate under strict, enforceable regulations that put human well-being above profit. But more importantly, public ownership must replace private control in critical industries. Housing, healthcare, transportation, education, and energy, these are not commodities to be bought and sold by billionaires and hedge funds. They are human rights, and they must be reclaimed as such.

And then there is the issue of religious control, which has been one of the most effective tools of oppression for centuries. The perverts of theocracy have always understood that controlling belief is the key to controlling behavior. They use fear, guilt, and divine authority to justify hierarchy, enforce obedience, and convince the masses that suffering is righteous while resistance is sinful. They declare that poverty is a test of faith while they amass untold wealth. They claim to defend morality while covering up the abuse and corruption that runs through every level of their institutions.

If humanity is ever to heal, the grip of religious authoritarianism must be broken. Faith must be separated from power, stripped of its ability to dictate policy, removed from its influence over the courts, the schools, and the laws. No more special tax exemptions for churches that operate as political machines. No more religious doctrine creeping into public education, reproductive rights, or social policy. No more megachurch pastors using the pulpit to push political propaganda while living like kings off the money of the desperate and the deceived. Religion, if it is to exist at all, must be a personal belief, not a mechanism of control.

Because the reality is, every structure that enforces oppression, economic, corporate, religious, is tied together. They work in unison, reinforcing each other, ensuring that the power of the ruling class is never truly threatened. And that means fighting one aspect of the virus is not enough. The entire structure must be dismantled and something new must be built in its place.

This does not mean returning to an old system that failed. It cannot be another variation of capitalism dressed up in progressive language, another attempt at regulating exploitation instead of eradicating it. The solution must be radical because the destruction caused by the greed virus is radical. The solution must be transformative, because no half-measures will undo the damage that has been done. The solution must be driven by the people, not imposed from above, because only those who have suffered under this system truly understand what needs to change.

The greed virus thrives on the illusion that there is no alternative. That the systems we live under, where billionaires hoard wealth while the rest struggle, where corporations extract every ounce of value from workers and resources, where religious institutions dictate morality and law, are simply the natural order of things. This lie has been repeated for so long, reinforced through education, media, and politics, that many people can no longer imagine a different way of living. And that is exactly the point. The perverts in power, the economic elites, the political strongmen, the religious authoritarians, do not just control resources. They control imagination. They work tirelessly to ensure that people are incapable of envisioning a world in which they are not at the top.

Because once people do, once they start to see the systems for what they are, once they recognize that the suffering, the struggle, the exploitation are not inevitable but designed, the foundations of power begin to crack. Fighting the greed virus means more than just exposing corruption, redistributing wealth, or regulating corporate power. It means creating a fundamentally new way of organizing society, one that prioritizes human well-being over profit, sustainability over exploitation, cooperation over competition. And to do that, we must first unlearn the lies we've been told. We must break free from the mental prison that tells us there is no alternative. Because there is. There always has been.

Imagine a world where housing is not a speculative asset, where people are not evicted so hedge funds can buy up properties and jack up rents. Where no one lives in fear of homelessness because shelter is recognized as a basic human right, not a commodity to be exploited. This is not a utopian fantasy. It is an entirely achievable reality, if the power of landlords, real estate moguls, and financial speculators is dismantled. If land and housing are treated as public goods rather than investment opportunities. If communities take control of their own neighborhoods instead of leaving them in the hands of developers who see them only as numbers on a spreadsheet.

This has been done before. There are worker-owned housing cooperatives, community land trusts, publicly owned rental systems that exist outside of the market and function for the benefit of the people who live in them. The only reason these models are not widespread is because the greed virus ensures that property is concentrated in fewer and fewer hands, maximizing profit at the expense of human dignity.

And what about labor? The current system is built on the lie that work is a path to prosperity. That if people just work hard enough, they will be rewarded. But in reality, wages have stagnated for decades while corporate profits have skyrocketed. Productivity has increased, but that wealth has not gone to the workers, it has been funneled upward, extracted by executives and shareholders who do no labor themselves. The perverts running this system will tell you that this is just how the market works. That some inequality is necessary. That higher wages will destroy the economy. But these are lies, repeated endlessly to justify the theft of human labor.

A real solution means rejecting the idea that corporations should exist solely to generate profit for their owners. It means shifting from a system of private ownership to one where workers control the businesses they operate, where decisions are made democratically, where profit is not extracted from labor but reinvested into the communities that sustain it. Worker cooperatives exist all over the world, proving that this model is not only possible but far more sustainable and just than the corporate structure we live under now. The only thing preventing this shift is power, the entrenched power of those who benefit from a system of wage slavery.

Public ownership must extend beyond housing and labor. Every vital resource, energy, healthcare, transportation, education, must be removed from the hands of private industry and returned to the people. There is no logical reason that electricity, water, and internet access should be controlled by for-profit corporations that charge whatever they want while delivering subpar services. There is no reason that healthcare should be a financial burden, that medical bankruptcy should even exist, that people should have to choose between seeing a doctor and paying rent. There is no justification for an education system that saddles students with debt for decades while enriching university administrators and lenders. Every one of these industries operates under the same parasitic logic: extract as much wealth as possible, provide the least amount of

130

service necessary to keep people dependent, and make sure that alternatives are either nonexistent or inaccessible. And yet, around the world, there are examples of publicly owned and democratically run systems that function better than privatized ones. Universal healthcare, free higher education, publicly controlled utilities, these are not radical ideas. They already exist. They are simply kept out of reach for most people because the greed virus ensures that scarcity and suffering are more profitable than abundance and well-being.

Of course, the perverts who control these industries will fight tooth and nail to prevent any shift in power. They will scream about socialism, about big government, about inefficiency. But what is inefficient about a system that guarantees housing, healthcare, and education for all? What is inefficient about removing middlemen whose only purpose is to extract profit from people's basic needs? The current system is inefficient by design, not for the rich, not for the corporations, not for the elite, but for everyone else. It is designed to ensure that people are always on the brink of collapse, always struggling just enough to stay compliant, always too exhausted to fight back.

And that exhaustion is not just economic. It is political, it is cultural, it is existential. The greed virus does not just drain material resources, it drains hope. It ensures that people feel powerless, that they see politics as pointless, that they believe no real change is possible. And it is this aspect of the virus that must be fought as aggressively as the material conditions it creates. Because as long as people believe that there is no alternative, they will never fight for one.

That is why the battle is not just in policy, in economics, in legislation. It is in imagination. It is in showing people that another world is possible, that they do not have to accept the reality forced upon them by corporate and religious overlords. That society does not have to be structured around greed, around control, around hierarchy. That there are other ways of organizing life, ways that prioritize collective well-being over individual hoarding, ways that ensure security and dignity for all rather than unimaginable luxury for the few.

There is no single blueprint for this change. No one-size-fits-all solution. The transition from a system infected by the greed virus to one based on justice and sustainability will take many forms. Some solutions will be local, small-scale, community-driven. Others will be national, requiring legislative and institutional transformation. Some will be rapid, the result of crisis and uprising. Others will be slow, the product of gradual shifts in consciousness and political will. The point is not to prescribe one path but to make clear that *a path exists*. That people do not have to continue living under the thumb of corporate feudalism. That the world we live in now, the world of exploitation, inequality, and environmental destruction, is not inevitable.

The final step in fighting the greed virus is ensuring that those who have benefited from it, those who have hoarded wealth, stripped resources, enslaved workers, are never allowed to do so again. Wealth must not only be redistributed; it must be prevented from ever becoming concentrated in so few hands again. That means strict limits on corporate influence, on private property, on financial speculation. It means ensuring that religious institutions never again have the power to dictate policy or control people's lives. It means dismantling monopolies, breaking up the financial elite, and creating economic and political systems that cannot be hijacked by the perverts who have ruled for so long.

Because the ultimate truth is this: the greed virus is not natural. It is not an inherent part of human nature. It is a choice. It was built, piece by piece, by those who wanted power. And if it was built, it can be dismantled. If it was created, it can be destroyed. If it has ruled for generations, it can be overthrown.

And when it is, the world that comes after will not be one of scarcity, of suffering, of endless struggle. It will be one where people finally have the chance to *live*, not as commodities, not as laborers, not as subjects of a ruling class, but as free human beings. That is not utopian thinking. That is simply what justice looks like.

Fighting the greed virus is not just about dismantling the existing structures of power; it is about ensuring that they can never be rebuilt. The perverts who have controlled wealth, industry, government, and religion for generations will not willingly surrender their grip. They will adapt, evolve, and rebrand their oppression to fit the times. They have done it before. Every time the people have risen up to demand justice, they have found ways to co-opt the movement, to turn it into another means of control. That is why any real fight against the greed virus must not only focus on removing the ruling class but on making sure their entire system is permanently dismantled. The goal is not just to redistribute wealth or pass progressive laws; it is to prevent the conditions that allow this level of exploitation and hierarchy to exist in the first place.

That begins with removing the economic mechanisms that funnel wealth to the top. Capitalism, as it currently exists, is a system designed to consolidate resources, not distribute them. It thrives on scarcity, using artificial constraints on housing, wages, healthcare, and education to keep people desperate. The more desperate people are, the more control the system has over them. This is why poverty is not an accident but a feature of the system. It is why every gain made by workers is met with a backlash from those who own industry. They know that the moment people are secure, the moment they are not struggling just to survive, they start questioning everything. They start demanding more. They start realizing that they should have had power all along.

For this reason, the only real solution is an economic model that puts control in the hands of workers and communities rather than executives and shareholders. This means removing profit-driven motives from essential services. It means shifting from a system where private ownership dictates access to one where resources are shared, governed democratically, and used for public good rather than private accumulation. There are already examples of this working in small-scale models: worker-owned cooperatives, community-run food distribution networks, municipal-owned utilities that provide cheaper, more reliable services than their privatized counterparts. The only thing preventing these models from scaling is the chokehold of corporate control. The perverts who run the global economy know that once people see these alternatives working, their entire illusion begins to fall apart. That is why they fight so hard to ensure that alternatives are either demonized or destroyed before they can take hold.

Dismantling corporate power must go hand in hand with dismantling political corruption. The current system is not just about economic dominance, it is about ensuring that the mechanisms of democracy itself serve the interests of the ruling class. Every aspect of governance has been corrupted by money, from the way campaigns are funded to the way laws are written. The corporations and billionaires who profit off this system do not just rely on market forces; they rely on policies that protect their wealth and punish anyone who threatens it. This is why lobbying exists. It is why corporations can spend unlimited amounts of money on elections, ensuring that only candidates who serve their interests ever make it into positions of power. It is why regulations that protect workers, the environment, and consumers are either weakened or outright removed.

Any real fight against the greed virus requires ending the influence of money in politics. That means abolishing corporate donations, breaking up media monopolies, and ensuring that elections are no longer determined by which candidate can raise the most money from billionaires. It means fundamentally restructuring governance so that power is decentralized, preventing the creation of another ruling class under a different name.

134

But it is not just politics and economics that need to change.
The greed virus has infected every aspect of culture, shaping
the way people think, the way they see themselves and their
place in the world. From birth, people are conditioned to see
competition as natural, to accept hierarchy as inevitable, to
believe that suffering is the price of success. The American
Dream, the idea that anyone can succeed if they just work hard
enough, is one of the most effective lies ever told. It keeps
people blaming themselves for systemic problems, chasing
individual success rather than collective liberation.

Breaking this conditioning is as important as breaking
economic and political control. A truly free society requires not
just new structures of governance but new ways of thinking.
People must unlearn the false narratives they have been fed.
They must reject the notion that success is measured by wealth,
that human worth is tied to productivity, that competition is
the only path forward.

That is why education must be radically transformed. Schools
must stop functioning as factories designed to produce obedient
workers for a corporate economy. They must become centers
of critical thought, where students learn not just facts but how
to recognize exploitation. History must be taught in its entirety,
not sanitized to erase the crimes of the ruling class. Economics
must be reframed to show that capitalism is not the only
option, that alternative models exist and have succeeded.
Media literacy must be prioritized, ensuring that people
understand how propaganda works.

And finally, the fight against the greed virus must include a
complete restructuring of our relationship with the planet. The
same forces that have hoarded wealth and destroyed
democracy have turned the Earth into an open-air factory,
extracting resources without concern for sustainability,
poisoning land and water, pushing ecosystems to collapse in the
pursuit of infinite profit. Climate collapse is not separate from
economic and political collapse, it is a symptom of the same

disease. The billionaires buying up land in New Zealand, building private bunkers, and stockpiling resources are doing so because they know what they have done. They are preparing to survive the catastrophe they created while leaving the rest of humanity to suffer its consequences.

Healing the world means shifting from extraction to regeneration, from endless consumption to sustainable stewardship. It means putting land and water back under the control of the people who live on it, rather than corporations that see it only as profit. It means recognizing that the survival of the planet is the survival of humanity.

The fight against the greed virus is not just a political or economic struggle. It is a cultural, psychological, and existential battle for the survival of humanity. It requires unlearning everything the ruling class has conditioned people to believe. It requires a total rejection of their values, their priorities, their vision of the world.

Because it is not. A world free from the greed virus is not only possible, it is necessary. The perverts in power may believe they are untouchable, but they are not. Their system only works as long as people accept it. And once people decide to reject it, to refuse to be ruled, to demand something better, to build something new, their power crumbles.

Special Note: The Greatest Wealth Heist in History— How They Stole It All

Since the 1980s, the ruling class has pulled off the most audacious act of wealth redistribution in modern history, but not in the way they like to frame it. They scream about the horrors of socialism, about how redistributing wealth from the rich to the people is theft. But they have spent the last four decades doing exactly that in reverse, redistributing *trillions* from the bottom 90% to the top 1%, stripping workers, communities, and public institutions of resources while stuffing their pockets with the spoils.

Reaganomics, neoliberalism, trickle-down economics, whatever branding they slap on it, the goal has always been the same: steal from the people and give to the rich. In 1980, the wealthiest 1% of Americans controlled about 10% of the nation's wealth. By 2023, they controlled over 30%. Meanwhile, wages stagnated, job security collapsed, unions were gutted, and the cost of everything, healthcare, housing, education, skyrocketed, all while CEOs and hedge fund managers reaped the profits. Between 1979 and 2021, the bottom 90% of Americans saw their real wages grow by just 15%. The top 1%? Over 400%.

And how did they pull it off? Through a relentless, systematic looting of the public. First, they slashed taxes for the ultra-rich, Reagan's first major tax cut reduced the top income tax rate from 70% to 28%, ensuring billionaires and corporations kept more of their hoarded wealth while the rest of the country picked up the tab. Then they went after labor, outsourcing jobs, breaking unions, and turning stable employment into precarious, low-wage gig work. They deregulated industries, letting corporations profit at the expense of workers and the environment. They privatized public goods, from utilities to education to healthcare, so that even the most basic human needs became sources of profit extraction. And they gutted social safety nets, slashing welfare, public housing, and worker protections while handing out endless tax breaks and subsidies to the wealthy.

By 2020, the richest 1% had captured $50 trillion that once belonged to the bottom 90%. That's not market forces. That's theft. That's wealth redistribution, but from the poor to the rich. Every dollar taken from wages and turned into corporate profits, every home foreclosed and scooped up by private equity, every hospital bill inflated to line the pockets of executives, every school underfunded so billionaires could dodge taxes, that was wealth stolen from the people.

And now, they are preparing for the next phase: *techno-feudalism*.

The future they are building is not one of freedom, opportunity, or innovation. It is one where ownership of everything, land, housing, labor, technology, is consolidated into the hands of a small ruling class while the rest of the population becomes permanent renters, gig workers, and data slaves. They do not want capitalism as we have known it; they want neo-serfdom, a world where billionaires function as digital feudal lords, controlling not just the economy but the very fabric of reality itself.

Look at their investments: Elon Musk, Jeff Bezos, and Mark Zuckerberg aren't just buying companies, they're buying entire *infrastructures of control.* They want to own the roads, the internet, the satellites, the payment systems. They are positioning themselves as the architects of a future where every interaction, every transaction, every aspect of life flows through systems they control. Crypto? A digital playground for billionaires while the masses are pushed into government-controlled central bank digital currencies. AI? A tool to eliminate human labor while concentrating wealth in the hands of tech oligarchs. The metaverse? A digital plantation where people will work, socialize, and spend money in a world they do not own.

This is not speculation. This is their plan. The World Economic Forum openly talks about a future where "you will own nothing and be happy." But who does own everything? The same perverts who spent the last 40 years looting the world.

Techno-feudalism is not just an economic shift, it is a full-scale redesign of society, one where the people at the top do not even need governments anymore. They are building private cities, private currencies, private law enforcement. They are seceding from humanity while keeping the rest of us locked into digital fiefdoms. And just like in the last great wealth heist, they will sell this future as progress, as innovation, as inevitable.

But it is not inevitable. The people still outnumber them. Their power is fragile, it relies on the illusion that their control is permanent, that their monopolies cannot be broken. But they can be. The first step is exposing their plan. The second is refusing to participate. The third is reclaiming what was stolen, before they finish locking the doors behind them.

END
GREED
NO
MORE
CROAGS!
NO
MORE
perverts

~12
The Way Back is to FIGHT BACK NOW

There is no savior coming. No politician, no billionaire philanthropist, no moral authority is going to step in and fix this mess. The people in power, the hoarders, the perverts, the architects of greed and oppression, have no interest in change because the system works exactly as they designed it to. They are not misguided. They are not making mistakes. They are not failing at leadership. They are succeeding at domination. And the only way to undo their stranglehold is for the people they exploit to fight back with everything they have. Not tomorrow. Not in the next election cycle. Not when the "right" leader emerges. Now.

The way back to a just and livable world is through direct action, through the coordinated dismantling of every system that keeps us divided, weakened, and dependent on the very forces that destroy us. It means rejecting the fantasy that a broken system can be reformed. It means refusing to play by their rules, refusing to beg for table scraps, refusing to let the architects of our suffering dictate the terms of resistance. And it means fighting smarter, using every available tool, not just protest and civil disobedience, but technology, strategy, and collective power, to strike at the heart of the beast.

For too long, the powerful have relied on the masses being technologically illiterate, politically disorganized, and socially divided. They have built their empire on the assumption that people are too busy, too exhausted, too distracted to mount an effective opposition. They use AI to manipulate public opinion, to control narratives, to rewrite history in real time. They use blockchain to evade taxes, to launder money, to build decentralized power structures that operate beyond the reach of any government. They use surveillance to track dissenters, to anticipate revolts before they happen, to neutralize opposition before it can grow. They have used every technological advancement of the modern world to entrench their power, but what happens when those same tools are turned against them?

Imagine a resistance that moves as fast as their propaganda machines, that uses AI to deconstruct their lies in real time, that harnesses data to expose corruption before they can cover it up. Imagine a movement that doesn't just react to the abuses of power but anticipates them, disrupts them before they can take hold. The greed virus has survived because it has always been one step ahead, always shifting, adapting, mutating to maintain its grip. But modern technology has made it possible to outmaneuver them, to build a decentralized, intelligent, and relentless opposition that cannot be silenced, cannot be bought, and cannot be controlled.

This is the fight now. Not just in the streets, not just in the courts, but in the very systems they have used against us. The tools of oppression are also the tools of liberation, but only if people are willing to claim them. This means learning the language of power, coding, hacking, blockchain, AI, decentralized finance, encrypted communication, autonomous organization. This means creating parallel structures that exist beyond the reach of billionaires, beyond the grasp of governments that serve only the elite. It means using technology not just to expose their crimes but to build an alternative that renders their systems obsolete.

They expect resistance in the form of marches, strikes, petitions. And yes, those are necessary. But what they don't expect, what they fear, is the realization that their wealth, their control, their entire empire exists only because people allow it to. What happens when workers don't just strike, but seize control of industry? When renters don't just protest, but collectively refuse to pay? When entire populations stop accepting the legitimacy of a system that serves only the powerful?

This is the fight. And it requires imagination, courage, and the willingness to unlearn everything we have been conditioned to believe about power.

Because here's the truth: they are not invincible.

They have built a world that convinces people otherwise, a world where billionaires seem untouchable, where corrupt politicians appear above the law, where corporations function like unchallenged gods dictating the terms of human survival. But this illusion only holds as long as people believe in it. The moment people stop playing along, the whole thing begins to unravel.

This is why they use fear. Fear of poverty, fear of imprisonment, fear of social exclusion. Fear is their primary weapon. But fear only works when people believe they have something left to lose. And the reality is that under this system, people are already losing everything. Housing, healthcare, dignity, the future of the planet itself, what is left to protect, except the illusion of safety?

The alternative to fighting back is not peace. It is not stability. It is obliteration. It is a world where billionaires build private fortresses while the rest drown in rising oceans, burn in corporate-engineered wildfires, starve while food supplies are controlled by hedge funds. It is a world where automation replaces workers, where every job becomes gig labor, where a permanent underclass is expected to suffer in silence while the elite extract the last remnants of wealth from the planet. And this isn't a dystopian fantasy. It's already happening.

Every law passed in the last two decades has made this future more certain. Every billionaire's tax cut, every rollback of worker protections, every expansion of private control over public resources. They are accelerating toward a world where democracy is a relic, where the wealthy are untouchable, where the masses are too broken to resist. But they are wrong to assume they cannot be stopped.

They have underestimated human resilience. They have underestimated what happens when people reach their breaking point and realize there is no other option but to fight. They have underestimated the sheer, raw power of collective action, of strategic defiance, of relentless resistance. And they will regret it.

The time for half-measures is over. The time for asking nicely, for waiting for justice, for hoping that things will improve on their own, is done. The perverts who run this world are not waiting. They are not hesitating. They are not debating whether they should take more. They are already doing it. And that means the response must be immediate, overwhelming, and uncompromising.

No more playing by their rules. No more waiting for politicians to grow a conscience. No more pretending that voting is enough. The way back to a world that is livable, just, and free is through a fight that they cannot contain, cannot co-opt, and cannot recover from.

The way back is through:

- Disrupting every system they use to maintain control. If corporations run the world, they must be made to fail. If billionaires hoard wealth, that wealth must be taken. If religious institutions push oppression, their power must be stripped.

•	Using their own technology against them. The tools they built to control can be turned into weapons of liberation. AI to deconstruct their propaganda. Hacking to expose their crimes. Blockchain to create financial systems beyond their control.

•	Finding allies in each other, not in politicians. Politicians exist to serve power. They will not save anyone. The only way forward is through direct action, through mutual aid, through the collective realization that we do not need them.

•	Conceiving a new way of being, living, and loving. A world beyond hierarchy, beyond greed, beyond the parasitic structures that have dictated human existence for far too long. A world where power is decentralized, where resources are shared, where survival is not a privilege for the few but a guarantee for all.

This future is possible. But it will not be handed to us. It must be built, fought for, taken. Because the alternative is letting them win. And that is not an option. Not now. Not ever.

Fighting back is not just a choice, it is survival. The ruling class, the corporate overlords, the religious zealots propping up this system of greed and oppression, they do not care if people suffer. They do not care if entire communities collapse, if the planet becomes uninhabitable, if generations to come inherit nothing but a wasteland of debt, disease, and despair. They care only about one thing: maintaining their control. And as long as people obey, as long as they accept the crumbs thrown to them, as long as they remain distracted by the circus of media and political theater, the perverts who run this world will continue to strip it for parts, hoarding what remains for themselves while telling everyone else there is simply not enough to go around.

But there is enough. There has always been enough. The world is not suffering from a lack of resources, it is suffering from hoarding. From the grotesque consolidation of wealth and power into the hands of the very few. Food shortages, housing crises, unaffordable healthcare, failing infrastructure, these are not accidents. They are not inevitable. They are deliberate, designed to create dependency, to ensure that people remain too desperate, too exhausted, too demoralized to fight back. This is why the system is not simply inefficient, it is working exactly as it was built to work. And it is why dismantling it requires more than protests, more than petitions, more than a few well-meaning reforms. It requires a fundamental restructuring of power itself.

That starts with rejecting the myth that billionaires and corporations are untouchable. They want the public to believe that their wealth is protected by some divine law, that they have earned their power, that the system cannot function without them. But this is a lie. They have not built wealth, they have extracted it. They do not create, they consume. Every industry they claim to control, housing, healthcare, technology, food production, functions only because workers make it function. And the moment workers recognize their true power, the game changes.

Imagine if workers across entire industries refused to comply. If the people who run hospitals, deliver goods, grow food, and maintain infrastructure decided they would no longer uphold a system that exploits them. If labor ceased to be a bargaining chip for the rich, if corporations were no longer able to profit from stolen wages, if the wealth they have hoarded was reclaimed not through negotiation but through direct action. This is the power they fear most. Not an election. Not a new law. Not a progressive politician talking about fairness. They fear the realization that they cannot rule without the consent of the people they exploit.

146

And that consent is breaking. People are beginning to see through the illusion, recognizing that the world does not have to function this way, that better alternatives exist. That means breaking the financial stranglehold that allows corporations to dictate policy. It means replacing a stock market economy with one that prioritizes human needs rather than investor profits. It means redistributing land, returning stolen wealth, ensuring that resources like food, energy, and water are no longer controlled by private interests but belong to the people who rely on them.

This is not an unrealistic dream. The only reason it sounds radical is because the ruling class has spent decades convincing the public that justice is impossible, that collective ownership is unworkable, that capitalism is the natural state of humanity. They have erased history, burying examples of societies that have functioned without their parasitic control. They have conditioned people to believe that without billionaires, without landlords, without private industry, the world would descend into chaos. But the truth is that their version of order, this system of constant exploitation, of artificial scarcity, of endless inequality, is the real chaos. It is why people are overworked and underpaid. It is why families are homeless while thousands of apartments sit empty. It is why people die of preventable diseases while pharmaceutical companies rake in billions. The world does not need them. They need the world to believe it does.

And the first step to breaking that illusion is learning how to fight with more than just slogans and outrage. The perverts in power have spent centuries perfecting their ability to suppress rebellion. They have built surveillance systems that track dissenters, propaganda networks that rewrite history in real time, law enforcement agencies designed not to protect the public but to defend private capital. They use technology to reinforce their rule, to monitor, to manipulate, to control. And for too long, people have been forced to play defense, reacting to oppression rather than actively dismantling it. But that is changing. The same technological advancements they have used to entrench their power can be used against them.

Decentralized networks. Encrypted communication. Blockchain infrastructure that allows wealth to be transferred outside of their financial institutions. AI-driven analysis that exposes their propaganda before it can take hold. Data collection that tracks and documents their corruption, preventing them from rewriting history when the consequences of their actions become undeniable. The very systems they have built to maintain control can be repurposed, weaponized against them, used to create an alternative that operates beyond their reach.

This is what they fear most, not just opposition, but opposition that is intelligent, organized, and impossible to contain. Protests can be shut down. Elections can be rigged. Social movements can be infiltrated, co-opted, turned into performative spectacles that achieve nothing beyond symbolic victories. But a decentralized, tech-savvy resistance that builds its own systems outside of their control? That is something they cannot stop. It does not rely on politicians, on institutions, on the slow, bureaucratic process of appealing to a system that was never built to serve the people in the first place. It is direct, immediate, and irreversible.

And this does not just apply to economics. It applies to every aspect of society. Education, for example, has been turned into a tool for control, a means of ensuring that people do not question their place in the hierarchy. Public schools are systematically defunded, while private institutions thrive, ensuring that the best education is only available to those who can afford it. Student debt is used as a modern form of indentured servitude, trapping entire generations in financial servitude before they ever have a chance to build a life for themselves. But what happens when people refuse? When education is democratized, when knowledge is made freely available, when learning is no longer a commodity to be

148

bought and sold but a right that belongs to everyone? When AI and open-source platforms replace predatory universities, ensuring that no one ever has to pay for access to information again?

The same applies to healthcare. The greed virus ensures that medical treatment is available only to those who can afford it, that life-saving drugs are priced out of reach, that hospitals function like corporations rather than public institutions. But this does not have to be the case. Technology has made it possible to break the pharmaceutical monopoly, to decentralize medical knowledge, to provide universal access to healthcare without relying on private insurance or government bureaucracy. The only reason it has not happened is because the perverts who control the industry profit more from sickness than from health.

This is what fighting back means. Not just resisting their policies but creating an entirely new way of living that does not require their approval, their institutions, or their systems of control. It means refusing to play by their rules, refusing to engage with their political theater, refusing to accept the limitations they have placed on what is possible.

Because the truth is, everything they have built is fragile. Their wealth, their power, their entire empire is held together by the illusion that people cannot survive without them. That people will continue working, continue obeying, continue submitting because they have no other choice. But they do. And once enough people realize that, once they stop believing in the inevitability of their own oppression, the game is over.

The way back is through relentless, uncompromising defiance. It is through the creation of alternative systems, through the rejection of corporate rule, through the realization that the world does not belong to the rich, to the politicians, to the theocrats. It belongs to the people. And they can take it back.

Not someday. Not in the distant future. Now.

The struggle against the greed virus is not just about tearing down what exists, it is about ensuring that what comes next is fundamentally different. The mistake of past revolutions has always been assuming that winning the fight is enough, that once the tyrants are removed, justice will naturally follow. But history is full of examples where power simply reshaped itself, where new rulers emerged to take the place of the old, where the people who sacrificed everything were left with nothing but a different flavor of the same oppression. The ruling class understands how to survive defeat. They wait. They adapt. They rebrand. If there is one thing the perverts and the hoarders excel at, it is burrowing into the next system like parasites, waiting for their chance to reclaim power. This is why the battle is not just about resistance, it is about ensuring that once they fall, they never rise again.

That means the revolution cannot just be about rage. It must be about construction. It must be about answering the question: what does the world look like once the billionaires, the corporate overlords, the religious tyrants, and the political frauds have been stripped of power? What replaces the systems they built? Because the old way, the assumption that democracy, left to its own devices, will naturally produce justice, is a lie. Democracy under capitalism was always an illusion. People voted, but their choices were preselected by wealth. They participated, but their labor was still exploited. They followed the law, but the law was always written to protect the powerful. A new world cannot be built on the remnants of this broken system. It must be something entirely different.

The first step is eliminating economic hierarchy. No more billionaires. No more monopolies. No more private ownership of resources that belong to all. The future must be built on shared wealth, on the understanding that land, water, food, housing, and healthcare are not privileges but collective rights.

150

That means moving beyond wage labor and into worker control. If people build the economy, they must own it. No more CEOs extracting billions while workers starve. No more landlords dictating the price of shelter. The very concept of hoarding wealth must be eradicated because hoarding is violence. When one person accumulates more than they need while millions suffer, they are committing an act of war against the people. The solution is not to tax them. It is to make sure wealth is never concentrated in their hands again.

Technology must also be liberated from private control. The digital world has been claimed by a handful of billionaires who use it to surveil, manipulate, and monetize every aspect of life. This cannot be allowed to continue. AI, blockchain, automation, these are tools that can be used to decentralize power, to ensure that no single entity can ever again dictate the flow of information, resources, or social structure. Imagine a world where news is no longer controlled by corporate interests, where money is no longer funneled through banks that extract wealth without contributing anything to society, where governance is fully transparent, immutable, and unhackable because it exists in decentralized, blockchain-based systems that no billionaire can alter. This is not some utopian fantasy. It is a reality that can be built if people refuse to allow the ruling class to monopolize the tools of the future.

Education must be restructured, because ignorance is one of the greatest weapons of oppression. The current system does not teach people how to think, it teaches them how to obey. The future must reject this entirely. Education must be free, global, and centered on critical thinking, history, and technology, not just memorization of the status quo. It must teach people how to resist manipulation, how to organize, how to build and sustain decentralized systems. Because revolutions do not last when the next generation is taught to rebuild the old world all over again.

Governance itself must be reimagined. The state, in its current form, is nothing more than a machine designed to enforce class rule. It exists to maintain wealth inequality, to protect the powerful from the people, to ensure that corporate and religious interests are never truly threatened. This is why reforming it has never worked. The state is not a neutral force; it is an instrument of oppression. The only path forward is to dismantle it and replace it with systems that do not concentrate power in a central authority. Governance must be local, direct, participatory. People must make decisions for themselves, in their own communities, without middlemen who can be bribed, lobbied, or corrupted. This is not lawlessness, it is democracy in its purest form.

Law enforcement, as it exists now, must also be abolished. Police forces were never designed to protect the people. They were designed to protect property, to crush uprisings, to enforce the will of the ruling class. They exist not to prevent harm but to ensure that harm is only committed by the right people, those in power. A just world does not need militarized enforcers who answer only to the wealthy. It needs community-based justice, harm reduction, accountability systems that are built on restoration rather than punishment. The prison-industrial complex must be torn down, because no society that cages human beings for profit can ever call itself civilized.

None of this will happen by accident. None of it will be given freely. Every step toward this world will be fought, violently, by those who benefit from the current system. The perverts in power will not surrender. They will not give up their wealth, their control, their ability to shape reality to serve their own interests. They will resist at every turn. They will unleash propaganda, police, military forces, economic warfare, and digital censorship. They will try to buy time, to stall, to negotiate, to convince people that half-measures are enough. They will try to make resistance seem futile, to convince people that their power is too great, that nothing can truly change.

But they are wrong.

Because once people recognize their own power, once they stop
fearing the system and start seeing it for what it is, a house of
cards built on deception, upheld only by compliance, the entire
structure begins to collapse. Once people stop obeying, stop
accepting, stop believing in the legitimacy of the ruling class,
their power disappears overnight. The final stage of revolution
is not just dismantling oppression. It is ensuring that it never
returns. It is creating a world where no one can ever again
hoard wealth, dictate laws, control bodies, or extract labor for
profit. It is building something that cannot be bought, cannot
be corrupted, cannot be overtaken by the same forces we are
fighting now.

This is not a dream. It is a necessity. The world cannot survive
under the greed virus. Humanity cannot thrive under
capitalism, under religious authoritarianism, under corporate
feudalism. The perverts who have ruled for centuries have
driven the planet to the edge of collapse. And now it is time to
take it back. Not just for today. Not just for the next election
cycle. But forever. Because if the people rise, if they organize, if
they refuse to go back to a system of greed and hierarchy, the
ruling class will never recover.

And once they are gone, once their empire is reduced to dust,
humanity will finally have a chance to live, not as subjects, not
as laborers, not as pawns in their game, but as free people. And
that will be the beginning of a world truly worth fighting for.

Never Forget Who the Enemy is & What They Are Capable of—Forced Birth

Cruelty is the Point—This is Who They Are

The imposition of forced birth laws is not about protecting life. It is about control. It is about using the machinery of the state to strip women and girls of autonomy, to reduce them to vessels for reproduction, ensuring their bodies remain subject to the authority of politicians, religious extremists, and corporate interests that profit from their oppression. These laws, enforced by people who champion capital punishment, defund education, and strip healthcare access, are not about life. They are about dominance. They remind half the population that their rights are conditional, revocable, and subject to the whims of an ideology that sees them as walking wombs.

In states like Ohio, this perverse logic has reached its most grotesque conclusion. A child, too young to legally consent to sex, too young to comprehend the violence inflicted upon her, is expected to carry a pregnancy to term as though it were some kind of divine obligation rather than a state-sanctioned horror. The case of a 10-year-old rape victim forced to flee Ohio for medical care was not an aberration. It was the inevitable consequence of a system designed to be deliberately cruel. The people who passed these laws knew the suffering they would cause. They knew that children would be trapped. And they did it anyway.

The forced birth movement does not care about the lives of these girls. It does not care that forcing a child to carry a pregnancy to term is medical abuse, that pregnancy in young girls carries life-threatening risks, or that childbirth is one of the leading causes of death among minors. This movement's purpose is not to protect, it is to punish. It enforces the idea that sex has consequences, and for women and girls, that consequence is subjugation. Reproductive autonomy is not a right but a privilege, granted only to those with the means and connections to bypass restrictions.

Forced birth is state-sponsored violence. It is an ideological project to roll back every gain women have made in the past century. It will not stop at abortion bans. It never does. The same people pushing these laws are fighting against contraception access, protections for domestic violence victims, and healthcare for mothers and children. If this were about children, the same lawmakers pushing these bans would be fighting for healthcare, childcare, and maternal support. Instead, they are doing the opposite, cutting funding for food assistance, restricting contraception, and ensuring poor women have fewer resources while forcing them to give birth.

Ohio has become one of the clearest examples of how forced birth laws function, not as policies to protect life, but as mechanisms of deliberate cruelty. The case of the 10-year-old girl forced to flee the state for an abortion sent shockwaves through the country, but not to the lawmakers who passed these bans. They knew this would happen. They knew that their laws made no exceptions for rape and incest. They knew that victims like this girl would be further victimized by a system that treated them as ideological sacrifices. And they did it anyway.

When she left the state for an abortion, right-wing media scrambled to discredit the story rather than face the reality of their policies. They questioned whether the case was real, accused doctors of fabricating it, and blamed journalists for

156

exposing the truth. When the facts became undeniable, they shifted tactics, going after the doctor who treated her, calling for prosecutions, making it clear that anyone who helps victims escape these laws will be punished.

This is the reality of forced birth laws. They do not just trap women and girls in unwanted pregnancies, they criminalize those who try to help them. Ohio and other states with near-total bans have created an environment where medical professionals fear criminal charges and the loss of their licenses for performing even life-saving procedures. The result is that healthcare decisions are not made by doctors and patients but by politicians, lawyers, and religious extremists who have hijacked the law to enforce their ideology.

Ohio's six-week abortion ban, a policy so extreme that many women do not even realize they are pregnant before the window closes, has already resulted in numerous cases of women being denied life-saving medical care. Patients experiencing miscarriages, sepsis, and other pregnancy complications have been turned away from hospitals, forced to wait until they are sick enough to legally qualify for an abortion. Women with nonviable pregnancies, fetuses diagnosed with fatal conditions, are told they must carry to term anyway, forced to endure months of physical and emotional agony for the sake of a law written by men who will never experience pregnancy. The law makes no distinction between hope and devastation. It forces suffering upon all.

Christian nationalism has always been a tool of oppression, but in the modern era, it has become a weapon for enforcing forced birth laws and subjugating women. The Ohio case and others like it are not isolated—they are the result of a long, calculated effort by religious extremists to dismantle bodily autonomy under the guise of morality. This is not about faith. It is about power. It is about using religion as a shield to justify stripping away rights, forcing an entire population to live under laws dictated by a fanatical minority.

The language they use is designed to mask their true intentions. They call themselves "pro-life," but their policies reveal a deep contempt for life, particularly the lives of women, children, and the poor. They insist that every embryo is sacred, but once that child is born, they disappear. They demand forced births but refuse to support paid parental leave, childcare, or living wages. In their world, life matters only until the moment of birth, after that, the burden is placed entirely on the mother. This is not morality. It is cruelty wrapped in piety, a perversion of faith designed to justify domination.

Forced birth policies are always championed by those who will never face the consequences of pregnancy. The lawmakers who craft these bans, the religious fundamentalists who lobby for their passage, the conservative judges who uphold them, they all have one thing in common: none of them will ever be forced to carry a pregnancy against their will. They will never have their bodies hijacked by a system that sees them as incubators rather than human beings. And because they will never experience any of these things, they feel entitled to dictate the reproductive lives of others.

The perversion of morality that fuels the forced birth movement is nowhere more apparent than in the way they respond to the suffering they create. They celebrate when abortion clinics close, when access to reproductive healthcare is stripped away, when desperate women and girls are left with no options. And when confronted with the horror stories, the children forced to give birth, the women who die because they were denied care, the families plunged into poverty, they refuse to take responsibility. They dismiss the suffering as unfortunate but necessary. In their eyes, suffering is not just collateral damage. It is the entire point.

Forced birth is about control, enforced through fear. The movement thrives on intimidation, on the knowledge that if people are terrified enough, of social stigma, criminal prosecution, financial ruin, they will comply. They criminalize doctors. They push civil lawsuits against anyone who helps a person obtain an abortion. They turn neighbors and even family members into informants. They spread misinformation, claiming abortion is dangerous, that it causes infertility, that it leads to regret, when in reality, the vast majority of people who have abortions do so because they know what is best for their own lives.

And the forced birth movement does not stop at abortion. Once they have stripped away reproductive rights, they move to contraception. They argue that IUDs and emergency contraception are "abortifacients," despite all medical evidence to the contrary. They push abstinence-only education, ensuring that young people are denied the knowledge they need to protect themselves. They insist that sex must have consequences, that pregnancy is a punishment, that women who seek control over their own reproduction are morally corrupt.

But forced birth is not just a women's issue. It is a human rights issue, a workers' rights issue, an economic justice issue, a healthcare issue, a racial justice issue. The people most impacted by abortion bans are the same people who are already marginalized, low-income workers, people of color, victims of domestic abuse, those living in conservative states with little access to healthcare. These laws do not impact the wealthy, the politicians who pass them, or the megachurch pastors who preach about the sanctity of life while living in tax-exempt mansions. They impact those with the least power and the least resources.

Make no mistake, this is a trap. The goal is not just to ban abortion. It is to make women economically dependent, to keep them tethered to marriages they might otherwise leave, to ensure they remain locked into cycles of poverty and subjugation. It is to create a system where women are forced to rely on men, the state, and religious institutions rather than determining the course of their own lives. And it is working.

States with the strictest abortion bans have also seen increases in maternal mortality, child poverty, and economic insecurity. The architects of these laws know this. That is precisely why they fight so hard to keep it that way.

But they are not invincible. The forced birth movement is built on a fragile foundation, on lies, on fear, on the assumption that people will not fight back. But people are fighting back. They are organizing, mobilizing, refusing to accept a future where their rights are dictated by religious extremists and political opportunists. They are exposing the hypocrisy, the cruelty, the fundamentally anti-life nature of these laws. They are reminding the world that forced birth is not an inevitability, it is a policy choice, and policies can be undone.

The only way to stop this movement is to confront it at every level. To fight it in the courts, in the streets, in workplaces, in homes. To refuse to allow their vision for the future to go unchallenged. To reject their lies, expose their motives, and demand not just the restoration of abortion rights but the expansion of reproductive justice. That means not just legal abortion, but accessible abortion. Not just birth control, but free and universal contraception. Not just protections for doctors, but full decriminalization of reproductive healthcare. This is not just about undoing past damage, it is about ensuring that no one is ever forced to carry a pregnancy they do not want.

The forced birth movement has made one thing clear: they will not stop on their own. They will not be swayed by reason, by compassion, by the overwhelming evidence that their policies cause harm. They will push forward until they are stopped. And the only people who can stop them are the ones who refuse to live under their rule. The ones who understand that freedom is not something given, it is something fought for, seized, and defended. Because if they are not stopped now, they will not stop at all. And if they win, the suffering we have already seen will be just the beginning.

The forced birth movement will not stop unless it is stopped. It has never been about life, it has always been about power, about keeping women, girls, and marginalized communities under control. Every policy, every law, every restriction is designed to strip away autonomy, to make reproductive decisions the domain of the state, the church, and the wealthy elite who will never suffer the consequences of their cruelty. This is not a debate. It is a war on freedom, dignity, and self-determination. The only way forward is through relentless opposition. Through exposing the lies, rejecting their authority, and fighting back at every level. Abortion rights, contraception access, reproductive justice, these are not privileges, they are fundamental human rights. And they will not be surrendered without a fight.

And despite their relentless claims of moral superiority, the hypocrisy of the forced birth movement is staggering. These same politicians who demand that every pregnancy be carried to term are the ones slashing funding for maternal healthcare, ensuring that the U.S. maintains one of the highest maternal mortality rates in the developed world. They fight against universal childcare, against paid family leave, against policies that would actually support the children they claim to care so much about. They are the same people who oppose expanding Medicaid, who cut funding for food assistance, who refuse to raise the minimum wage while insisting that single mothers should simply "work harder." They do not care about life. They care about control.

This perverse logic extends beyond abortion. These same lawmakers fight against laws that protect women from domestic violence. They oppose restrictions on child marriage, ensuring that grown men can continue to exploit young girls under the legal protection of marriage laws. They push policies that make it harder for victims of sexual assault to seek justice, ensuring that rapists are shielded while their victims are punished. They defend men like Brett Kavanaugh and Donald Trump, rallying behind them despite multiple credible allegations of sexual misconduct, while demonizing any woman who dares to speak out. They celebrate the punishment of women while rewarding the men who harm them. This is not morality. This is systemic abuse enshrined into law.

And the suffering extends far beyond the women and girls directly affected by these policies. The economic impact of forced birth laws is devastating, particularly for poor and working-class communities. The inability to access abortion means more families trapped in cycles of poverty, more children born into unstable homes, more women forced to leave school or quit their jobs because they have no choice but to carry unwanted pregnancies to term. It means more strain on healthcare systems, more children in foster care, more preventable deaths. These are not unintended consequences. They are the inevitable outcomes of a system designed to punish, to subjugate, to ensure that reproductive autonomy remains a privilege of the wealthy while the rest are bound by laws they had no hand in creating.

And yet, for all their cruelty, the forced birth movement has succeeded in one thing, it has made its agenda unmistakably clear. It has shown, with absolute certainty, that its goal is not life but domination. That its concern is not children but control. That its guiding principle is not morality but power. And that means there is no compromising with these forces. There is no reasoning with people who believe they have the right to dictate what happens in someone else's body. There is no middle ground with those who see pregnancy not as a medical condition but as a punishment for existing outside their rigid moral code. The only path forward is to dismantle the structures that allow these people to hold power in the first place.

This is not just a fight for abortion rights. It is a fight for freedom itself. It is a fight against religious authoritarianism, against patriarchal control, against a system that sees women and girls as second-class citizens whose bodily autonomy is negotiable. It is a fight against the growing movement to replace democracy with theocracy, to enshrine religious dogma into law, to strip away not just reproductive rights but every right that stands in the way of their ultimate goal, total domination of women's bodies, lives, and futures.

And it is a fight that cannot be won through elections alone. The politicians who pass these laws do not fear public opinion. They gerrymander districts, suppress votes, and stack the courts with judges who will uphold their agenda no matter how unpopular it is. They know that the vast majority of Americans support abortion rights, and they do not care. Because they do not answer to the people, they answer to the religious extremists and corporate donors who bankroll their campaigns. That means the only way to stop them is through direct action, through organized resistance, through relentless pressure that makes it clear that their power is illegitimate, their policies are unacceptable, and their vision for the future will not stand.

Because if history has shown anything, it is that these forces do not stop on their own. They do not suddenly realize their mistakes. They do not wake up one day and decide to respect human rights. They are stopped only when they are forced to stop. They are defeated only when they are confronted with an opposition too strong to ignore. And that opposition must come from everywhere, from the streets, from the courts, from workplaces, from communities, from every single person who refuses to accept a future dictated by theocrats and authoritarians.

Forced birth is not just an issue of reproductive rights. It is an issue of freedom, of democracy, of basic human dignity. It is the battle that will define this era, and the question is not whether people will fight back, it is whether they will do so before it is too late. Because the people behind these laws are not stopping. They are not slowing down. They are pushing harder, moving faster, and if they are not met with equal and opposite force, they will succeed in creating the world they dream of, a world where women are property, where rights exist only for those who conform, where theocracy replaces democracy, and where suffering is not an unfortunate consequence but the entire point.

There is a reason why forced birth policies are always championed by those who have never and will never face the consequences of pregnancy. The lawmakers who craft these draconian bans, the religious fundamentalists who lobby for their passage, the conservative judges who uphold them, they all have one thing in common: none of them will ever be forced to carry a pregnancy against their will. They will never have their bodies hijacked by a system that sees them as incubators rather than human beings. They will never wake up to find that the future they had planned has been stolen from them by a cruel and indifferent government. And because they will never experience any of these things, they feel entitled to dictate the reproductive lives of others, to enforce their rigid morality onto the bodies of those they see as undeserving of autonomy.

The perversion of morality that fuels the forced birth movement is nowhere more apparent than in the way they respond to the suffering they create. They celebrate when abortion clinics close, when access to reproductive healthcare is stripped away, when desperate women and girls are left with no options. They parade these victories as triumphs of righteousness, as if they have done something noble. And when confronted with the horror stories, the children forced to give birth, the women who die because they were denied life-saving care, the families plunged into poverty because they could not afford another mouth to feed, they refuse to take responsibility. They shift the blame. They dismiss the suffering as unfortunate but necessary. Because in their eyes, suffering is not just collateral damage. It is the entire point.

Forced birth is about control, and control is enforced through fear. The movement thrives on intimidation, on the knowledge that if people are terrified enough, of social stigma, of criminal prosecution, of financial ruin, they will comply. And so, they ensure that the consequences for seeking an abortion are as severe as possible. They criminalize doctors. They push measures that allow civil lawsuits against anyone who helps a person obtain an abortion. They introduce policies that encourage neighbors and even family members to report suspected abortions. They spread misinformation, claiming that abortion is dangerous, that it causes infertility, that it leads to regret and despair, when in reality, the vast majority of people who have abortions do so because they know what is best for their own lives.

And the forced birth movement does not stop at abortion. Once they have successfully stripped away reproductive rights, they move to contraception. They argue that IUDs and emergency contraception are "abortifacients," despite all medical evidence to the contrary. They frame birth control as an enabler of promiscuity, as something that allows women too much freedom, too much control over their own destinies. They push for abstinence-only education, ensuring that young people are denied the knowledge they need to protect themselves. They use the same rhetoric they have always used, that sex must have consequences, that pregnancy is a punishment, that women who seek to control their own reproduction are morally corrupt.

But forced birth is not just a women's issue. It is a human rights issue. It is a workers' rights issue, an economic justice issue, a healthcare issue, a racial justice issue. The people most impacted by abortion bans are the same people who are already marginalized, low-income workers, people of color, victims of domestic abuse, those living in conservative states with little access to healthcare. These laws do not impact the wealthy. They do not impact the politicians who pass them. They do not impact the megachurch pastors who preach about the sanctity of life while living in mansions funded by tax-exempt donations. They impact the people who have the least power, the least resources, the least ability to escape the trap that has been set for them.

And make no mistake, this is a trap. The goal is not just to ban abortion. The goal is to make women economically dependent, to keep them tethered to marriages they might otherwise leave, to ensure that they remain locked into cycles of poverty and subjugation. It is to create a system where women are forced to rely on men, on the state, on religious institutions, rather than being free to determine the course of their own lives. And it is working. States that have enacted the strictest abortion bans have also seen increases in maternal mortality, increases in child poverty, increases in economic insecurity. The architects of these laws know this. They know that when people are forced to give birth against their will, their futures are forever altered. And that is precisely why they fight so hard to keep it that way.

But they are not invincible. The forced birth movement is built on a fragile foundation, on lies, on fear, on the assumption that people will not fight back. But people are fighting back. They are organizing, mobilizing, refusing to accept a future where their rights are dictated by religious extremists and political opportunists. They are exposing the hypocrisy, the cruelty, the fundamentally anti-life nature of these laws. They are reminding the world that forced birth is not an inevitability, it is a policy choice, and policies can be undone.

The only way to stop this movement is to confront it at every level. To fight it in the courts, in the streets, in workplaces, in homes. To refuse to allow their vision for the future to go unchallenged. To reject their lies, to expose their motives, to demand not just the restoration of abortion rights but the expansion of reproductive justice in all its forms. That means not just legal abortion, but accessible abortion. Not just birth control, but free and universal access to contraception. Not just protections for doctors, but full decriminalization of reproductive healthcare. It means recognizing that this is not just about undoing the damage of the past, it is about ensuring that the future is one in which no one is forced to carry a pregnancy they do not want.

166

Because the forced birth movement has made one thing clear: they will not stop on their own. They will not be swayed by reason, by compassion, by the overwhelming evidence that their policies cause harm. They will push forward until they are stopped. And the only people who can stop them are the ones who refuse to live under their rule. The ones who understand that freedom is not something given, it is something fought for, something seized, something defended with every ounce of resistance that can be mustered. Because if they are not stopped now, they will not stop at all. And if they win, the suffering we have already seen will be just the beginning.

The forced birth movement will not stop unless it is stopped. It has never been about life, it has always been about power, about keeping women, girls, and marginalized communities under control. Every policy, every law, every restriction is designed to strip away autonomy, to make reproductive decisions the domain of the state, the church, and the wealthy elite who will never suffer the consequences of their cruelty. This is not a debate. It is a war on freedom, on dignity, on the right to self-determination. The only way forward is through relentless opposition. Through exposing the lies, rejecting their authority, and fighting back at every level. Abortion rights, contraception access, reproductive justice, these are not privileges, they are fundamental human rights. And they will not be surrendered without a fight.

Epilogue
Dare to Dream of a Post-Pervert Greed Virus World

They want you to believe this is the way the world has to be.
They want you to believe that their power is permanent, that
their wealth is untouchable, that their control is inevitable.
They want you to believe that no matter how hard you fight,
you will never win, because they have spent generations
making sure you never even dare to imagine a world without
them. But that is their greatest weakness. Because if you can
dream of something different, something better, something
beyond the greed and the suffering and the perversion of
morality that they have built, then you can create it. That is
what terrifies them the most. Not protests, not elections, not
policy reforms, but the raw, unstoppable force of human
imagination breaking free from the cage they have built around
it.

The greed virus is not invincible. The perverts who hoard
wealth, power, and resources at the expense of billions are not
gods. They are men, flesh and bone, sitting on thrones made of
stolen gold, clinging to a system that only survives because we
allow it to. And that is the truth they never want you to realize:
they are outnumbered. Their entire existence is built on convincing
the masses that resistance is futile, that the suffering they inflict
is natural, that the hierarchy they enforce is unshakable. But
history tells us otherwise. Every empire falls. Every ruling class
is eventually overthrown. Power never surrenders willingly, it
must be seized, taken, wrestled from the hands of those who
refuse to let it go. That is the fight before us. Not left versus
right, not liberal versus conservative, but the top versus the

bottom. The hoarders of wealth and power versus the people they have exploited for generations. This is class warfare, and the only question left is how long we are willing to suffer before we finally fight to win.

Because winning is possible. They do not want you to think so, but it is. Imagine a world where the billionaires are gone, where corporations do not own our governments, where people do not live in fear of medical debt, eviction, or starvation. Imagine a world where resources are shared, where work is meaningful, where no one is forced to trade their dignity for a paycheck that barely covers rent. Imagine a world where education is free, where healthcare is a right, where the planet is no longer treated as expendable for profit. Imagine a world where war is not waged for corporate gain, where the military does not exist to protect the wealth of the elite, where people are no longer disposable tools in their endless pursuit of more. Imagine a world where no child is forced into birth, where no person is owned by the state, where no law is written to uphold cruelty as righteousness.

That world is not some utopian fantasy. It is within reach. The only thing standing between us and that future is the greed of a tiny few who have convinced the many that such a future is impossible. They have stolen wealth, they have stolen power, and they have stolen imagination itself, erasing the idea that anything beyond this rigged system could ever exist. But they cannot stop us from dreaming. And once we begin to dream without limits, once we refuse to accept the artificial constraints they have placed on reality, then we begin to build.

And they will fight us. They will use everything they have to hold onto their stolen power. They will send their police, their armies, their courts. They will try to silence us, to imprison us, to break us. But they cannot win unless we let them. Because the numbers are on our side. The moment the people stop accepting their rule, it crumbles. The moment workers refuse to work for starvation wages, the economy halts. The moment

we reject their debt, their corporations, their manufactured
scarcity, they have nothing. *They need us more than we need them.*
That is the truth they have spent lifetimes trying to hide.

The future belongs to those who dare to take it. To those who
refuse to bow, who refuse to accept a world dictated by the
greed virus and the perverts who wield it. To those who are
willing to fight, not just with words, not just with votes, but with
every ounce of defiance that has been passed down through
generations of resistance. Power never surrenders without a
fight, but when it falls, it falls hard. And when we win, we will
not just inherit the world they left behind, we will build
something new, something better, something limitless.

Because if we can dream it, we can create it. And nothing
terrifies them more than that.

COURAGE IS CONTAGIOUS

TIDE—Target, Inspire, Disrupt, Empower—is not just a strategy; it is the way forward. The ruling class, the corporate parasites, and the religious extremists have built their power on a system designed to seem invincible. But it is not. Their control exists only because people allow it. The moment that changes, so does everything.

Target their foundations. Their wealth, their corporations, their false moral authority, all of it must be dismantled. If billionaires hoard, that wealth must be reclaimed. If religious institutions enforce oppression, their influence must be severed. They rely on people believing their rule is permanent. It is not.

Inspire the refusal to comply. They control through fear and hopelessness, selling the lie that change is impossible. But no empire lasts forever, and no system of oppression survives when people reject it. Show that a different world is not only possible but necessary.

Disrupt their mechanisms of control. The technology they built to oppress can be turned against them. AI to deconstruct their propaganda. Hacking to expose their corruption. Blockchain to create financial systems beyond their grasp. Their entire structure depends on obedience. Take that away, and it crumbles.

Empower people to build something better. They want dependence on politicians, corporations, and churches. But true power lies in communities, in mutual aid, in rejecting the need for rulers altogether. Their greatest fear is people realizing they do not need them.

This is the fight. The alternative is letting them win. That is not an option. The tide is rising, and when it crashes, the world they built on greed and control will not survive

List of Prints

About EATMS Productions

What's happening to women now is not random. It's structural.

Policy, culture, technology, and power are moving in the same direction.

EATMS maps them clearly and shows how to respond.

This title is part of an ongoing body of work. All EATMS Productions titles, across all series, authors, and formats, are components of a single connected project.

Start here: EATMS System Primer — Free Bundle
https://eatms.gumroad.com/l/dyvzbw

For full catalog or inquiries: eatms.me

Free survival booklet + EATMS updates: email "EATMS" to eatms@pm.me

Please feel free to burn part or all of this book, safely, as an effigy.